# What It Takes
## Writing in College

Laurence Behrens
*University of California*
*Santa Barbara*

Leonard J. Rosen
*Bentley College*

PEARSON
Longman

New York • San Francisco • Boston
London • Toronto • Sydney • Tokyo • Singapore • Madrid
Mexico City • Munich • Paris • Cape Town • Hong Kong • Montreal

*Executive Editor:* Suzanne Phelps Chambers
*Editorial Assistant:* Erica Schweitzer
*Senior Marketing Manager:* Sandra McGuire
*Production Manager:* Savoula Amanatidis
*Project Coordination and Text Design:* Elm Street Publishing Services
*Electronic Page Makeup:* Integra Software Services, Pvt. Ltd.

*Cover Design Manager:* Wendy Ann Fredericks
*Cover Designer:* Nancy Sacks
*Cover Photos:* Corbis Yellow Value RF/Corbis and Chris Cheadle/All Canada Photos/Getty Images
*Senior Manufacturing Buyer:* Dennis J. Para
*Printer and Binder:* Courier Corporation—Westford
*Cover Printer:* Coral Graphics Services, Inc.

For permission to use copyrighted material, grateful acknowledgment is made to the copyright holders on p. 172, which are hereby made part of this copyright page.

**Library of Congress Cataloging-in-Publication Data**
Behrens, Laurence.
    What it takes: writing in college/Laurence Behrens, Leonard J. Rosen.—1st ed.
       p. cm
    Includes bibliographical references and index.
    ISBN 978-0-205-64782-8
      1. English language—Rhetoric—Problems, exercises etc.
2. Report writing—Problems, exercises, etc.  3. Critical thinking—Problems, exercises, etc.  4. College readers.  I. Rosen, Leonard J. II. Title.

PE1408.B46928 2009
808'.042—dc22

                         2008028931

Please visit us at www.pearsonhighered.com

ISBN-13: 978-0-205-64782-8
ISBN-10: 0-205-64782-0

  5 6 7 8 9 10—CW—11 10 09

# Contents

*Preface*  vii

*A Note to the Student*  ix

**CHAPTER 1  Summary**  1

**What Is a Summary?**  1

**Can a Summary Be Objective?**  1

**Using the Summary**  2
  **Box:** Where Do We Find Written Summaries?  3

**The Reading Process**  4
  **Box:** Critical Reading for Summary  5

**How to Write Summaries**  7
  **Box:** Guidelines for Writing Summaries  7

**Demonstration: Summary**  8
  "Will Your Job Be Exported?"  9
    Alan S. Blinder
  Read, Reread, Highlight  17
  Divide into Stages of Thought  19
  Write a Brief Summary of Each Stage of Thought  21
  Write a Thesis: A Brief Summary of the Entire Passage  22
  Write the First Draft of the Summary  26
    Model Summary 1: *Combine Thesis Sentence with Brief
    Section Summaries*  26
  The Strategy of the Shorter Summary  27
    Model Summary 2: *Combine Thesis Sentence, Section Summaries,
    and Carefully Chosen Details*  28
  The Strategy of the Longer Summary  31

**How Long Should a Summary Be?**  32

**Avoiding Plagiarism**  33
  **Box:** Rules for Avoiding Plagiarism  36

**CHAPTER 2  Critical Reading and Critique**  37

**Critical Reading**  37

Question 1: To What Extent Does the Author Succeed
in His or Her Purpose?   38
**Box:** Where Do We Find Written Critiques?   38
Writing to Inform   39
   Evaluating Informative Writing   40
Writing to Persuade   41
   *Evaluating Persuasive Writing*   42
"We Are Not Created Equal in Every Way"   42
   Joan Ryan
   *Persuasive Strategies*   44
   *Logical Argumentation: Avoiding Logical Fallacies*   46
**Box:** Tone   49
Writing to Entertain   53
Question 2: To What Extent Do You Agree with the Author?   53
   *Identify Points of Agreement and Disagreement*   54
   *Explore the Reasons for Agreement and Disagreement:*
   *Evaluate Assumptions*   55

**Critique   57**
   **Box:** Guidelines for Writing Critiques   58
   How to Write Critiques   59

**Demonstration: Critique   60**
   To What Extent Does the Author Succeed in His or Her
      Purpose?   60
   To What Extent Do You Agree with the Author? Evaluate
      Assumptions.   61
   Model Critique: *A Critique of "We Are Not Created Equal in Every
      Way" by Joan Ryan*   62
   **Box:** Critical Reading for Critique   69
   The Strategy of the Critique   70

**CHAPTER 3 Synthesis   72**

**What Is a Synthesis?   72**

**Purpose   73**
   **Box:** Where Do We Find Written Syntheses?   73

**Using Your Sources   75**

**Types of Syntheses: Argument and Explanatory   76**
   **Explanation:** News Article from the *New York Times*   77
   **Argument:** Editorial from the *Boston Globe*   78

**How to Write Syntheses**    81
  **Box:** Guidelines for Writing Syntheses    82

**The Argument Synthesis**    84
  The Elements of Argument: Claim, Support, and Assumption    84

**Demonstration: Developing an Argument Synthesis—Balancing Privacy and Safety in the Wake of Virginia Tech**    86
  "Mass Shootings at Virginia Tech, April 16, 2007"    88
    **Virginia Tech Review Panel**
  "Virgina Tech Massacre Has Altered Campus Mental Health Systems"    93
    **Associated Press**
  The Family Educational Rights and Privacy Act    96
  Consider Your Purpose    98
  Making a Claim: Formulate a Thesis    99
  Decide How You Will Use Your Source Material    101
  Develop an Organizational Plan    101
  Formulate an Argument Strategy    103
  Draft and Revise Your Synthesis    104
  Model Synthesis: *Balancing Privacy and Safety in the Wake of Virginia Tech*    105
  The Strategy of the Argument Synthesis    115
  **Box:** Developing and Organizing Support for Your Arguments    122

**Developing and Organizing the Support for Your Arguments**    123
  Summarize, Paraphrase, and Quote Supporting Evidence    123
  Provide Various Types of Evidence and Motivational Appeals    124
  Use Climactic Order    124
  Use Logical or Conventional Order    125
  Present and Respond to Counterarguments    126
  Use Concession    126

**The Comparison-and-Contrast Synthesis**    127
  Organizing Comparison-and-Contrast Syntheses    128
    *Organizing by Source or Subject*    128
    *Organizing by Criteria*    129
  A Case for Comparison-and-Contrast: World War I and World War II    130
    *Comparison-and-Contrast (Organized by Criteria)*    130
  Model Exam Response    132
  The Strategy of the Exam Response    136
  Avoid Common Fallacies in Developing and Using Support    138

**The Explanatory Synthesis    138**
  Model Explanatory Synthesis    139
  The Strategy of the Explanatory Synthesis    142

**Summary    143**

**CHAPTER 4 Analysis    145**

**What Is an Analysis?    144**
  **Box:** Where Do We Find Written Analyses?    146

**Demonstration: Analysis    148**
  "The Plug-In Drug"    148
    Marie Winn
  Model Analysis: *The Coming Apart of a Dorm Society*    151

**How to Write Analyses    157**
  Consider Your Purpose    157
  Locate an Analytical Principle    158
  Formulate a Thesis    161
    *Part One of the Argument*    161
  **Box:** Guidelines for Writing Analysis    163
    *Part Two of the Argument*    164
  Develop an Organizational Plan    164
    *Turning Key Elements of a Principle or Definition into Questions*    165
    *Developing the Paragraph-by-Paragraph Logic of Your Paper*    165
  Draft and Revise Your Analysis    167
    *Write an Analysis, Not a Summary*    168
    *Make Your Analysis Systematic*    168
    *Answer the "So What?" Question*    168
    *Attribute Sources Appropriately*    169
  **Box:** Critical Reading for Analysis    169

**Analysis: A Tool for Understanding    170**

*Credits    172*

*Index    173*

*APA Documentation: Basic Formats    178*

*MLA Documentation: Basic Formats    179*

*Checklist Survey    182*

# Preface

*What It Takes: Writing in College* addresses four core skills that students should master to succeed as writers in college: the *summary*, the *critique*, the *synthesis*, and the *analysis*. The material here, in abbreviated form, constitutes the first part of *our Writing and Reading Across the Curriculum.* Over the past 28 years this text has helped writers new to academic settings to work with source materials and to generate competent, evidence-based papers across the disciplines.

Much of academic writing involves argument. Accordingly, *What It Takes* emphasizes the following:

- **The Elements of Argument: Claim, Support, and Assumption.** This section adapts the Toulmin approach to argument to the kinds of readings that students typically encounter when conducting research for their papers.

- **Developing and Organizing the Support for Your Arguments.** This section helps students to mine source materials for facts, expert opinions, and examples that will support their arguments.

- **Annotated Student Argument Paper.** A sample student paper highlights and discusses argumentative strategies that a student uses in drafting and developing a paper.

Throughout the text, we include boxed material that emphasizes the practical applications of writing summaries, syntheses, critiques, and analyses. The chapters are organized as follows:

## Chapter 1: Summary

Students are taken through the process of writing a summary of Alan S. Blinder's "Will Your Job be Exported?"—an economist's glimpse into the future of the global work force and the stability of American jobs. (Expect to be surprised.) We demonstrate how to annotate a source and divide it into sections, how to develop a thesis, and how to write and smoothly join section summaries.

## Chapter 2: Critical Reading and Critique

Chapter 2 offers a model critique on "We Are Not Created Equal in Every Way" by Joan Ryan, an op-ed that takes a strong view of parents who push their children at an early age to become professional dancers and athletes. The critique follows a set of guidelines for practicing critical reading.

## Chapter 3: Synthesis

Chapter 3 provides an argument synthesis on the topic of student privacy vs. campus safety in the wake of the Virginia Tech shootings. The argument synthesizes opinion pieces, newspaper and magazine articles, federal law, and an important investigative panel report. This section is followed by an example comparison-contrast synthesis, framed as a response to an exam question on World War I and World War II. The chapter concludes with excerpts from an explanatory synthesis on the subject of student privacy vs. campus safety, illustrating the differences between argumentation and explanation.

## Chapter 4: Analysis

The analysis chapter opens with brief, competing analyses of *The Wizard of Oz* that demonstrate how, employing different analytical principles (one psychoanalytic and the other political), two writers can read very different meanings into the classic children's book and movie. Following an example analysis by Marie Winn that examines excessive television viewing as an addiction ("The Plug-In Drug"), we present a student example of analysis: an application of a theory by the sociologist Randall Collins to living conditions in a college dormitory. We explain how to locate principles useful for conducting analyses, and we show how to write analyses themselves.

# A Note to the Student

Your sociology professor asks you to write a paper on attitudes toward the homeless population of an urban area near your campus. You are expected to consult books, articles, Web sites, and other online sources on the subject, and you are also encouraged to conduct surveys and interviews.

Your professor is making a number of assumptions about your capabilities. Among them:

- that you can research and assess the value of relevant sources;
- that you can comprehend college-level material, both print and electronic;
- that you can use theories and principles learned from one set of sources as tools to investigate other sources (or events, people, places, or things);
- that you can synthesize separate but related sources;
- that you can intelligently respond to such material.

These same assumptions underlie practically all college writing assignments. Your professors will expect you to demonstrate that you can read and understand not only textbooks but also critical articles and books, primary sources, Internet sources, online academic databases, and other material related to a particular subject of study. For example: For a paper on the progress of the Human Genome Project, you would probably look to articles and Internet sources for the most recent information. Using an online database, you would find articles on the subject in such print journals as *Nature*, *Journal of the American Medical Association*, and *Bioscience*, as well as in leading newspapers and magazines. A Web search engine might lead you to a useful site called "A New Gene Map of the Human Genome" <http://www. ncbi .nlm.nih.gov/genemap99/> and the site of the "Sequencing" section of the U.S. Department of Energy Joint Genome Institute <http://www.jgi/doe/gov/sequencing/index/html>.

You would be expected to assess the relevance of such sources to your topic and to draw from them the information and ideas you need. It's even possible that the final product of your research and reading may not be a conventional paper at all, but rather a Web site you create that explains the science behind the Human Genome Project, explores a particular controversy about the project, or describes the future benefits geneticists hope to derive from the project.

For a different class, you might be assigned a research paper on the films of the director Martin Scorsese. To get started, you might consult your film studies textbook, biographical sources on Scorsese, and anthologies of criticism. Instructor and peer feedback on a first draft might lead you to articles in both popular magazines (such as *Time*) and scholarly journals (such as *Literature/Film Quarterly*), a CD-ROM database (such as *Film Index International*), and relevant Web sites (such as the "Internet Movie Database" <http://us.imdb.com>).

These two assignment examples are very different, but the skills you need to work with them are the same. You must be able to research relevant sources. You must be able to read and comprehend those sources. You must be able to perceive the relationships among several pieces of source material. And you must be able to apply your own critical judgment to these various materials.

*What It Takes: Writing in College* provides you with the opportunity to practice the essential college-level skills we have just outlined and the forms of writing associated with them: the *summary*, the *critique*, the *synthesis*, and the *analysis*.

We hope that your writing course will serve as a kind of bridge to your other courses and that as a result of this work you will become more skillful at perceiving and expressing relationships among diverse topics. This little book can help you along your way. Because it involves such critical and widely applicable skills, your writing course may well turn out to be the most valuable—and one of the most interesting—of your academic career.

LAURENCE BEHRENS
LEONARD J. ROSEN

# 1

# Summary

## WHAT IS A SUMMARY?

The best way to demonstrate that you understand the information and the ideas in any piece of writing is to compose an accurate and clearly written summary of that piece. By a *summary* we mean a *brief restatement, in your own words, of the content of a passage* (a group of paragraphs, a chapter, an article, a book). This restatement should focus on the *central idea* of the passage. The briefest of summaries (one or two sentences) will do no more than this. A longer, more complete summary will indicate, in condensed form, the main points in the passage that support or explain the central idea. It will reflect the order in which these points are presented and the emphasis given to them. It may even include some important examples from the passage. But it will not include minor details. It will not repeat points simply for the purpose of emphasis. And it will not contain any of your own opinions or conclusions. A good summary, therefore, has three central qualities: *brevity, completeness,* and *objectivity.*

## CAN A SUMMARY BE OBJECTIVE?

Of course, the last quality mentioned above, objectivity, might be difficult to achieve in a summary. By definition, writing a summary requires you to select some aspects of the original and leave out others. Since deciding what to select and what to leave out calls for your personal judgment, your summary really is a work of interpretation.

And, certainly, your interpretation of a passage may differ from another person's.

One factor affecting the nature and quality of your interpretation is your *prior knowledge* of the subject. For example, if you're attempting to summarize an anthropological article and you're a novice in that field, then your summary of the article will likely differ from that of your professor, who has spent twenty years studying this particular area and whose judgment about what is more or less significant is undoubtedly more reliable than your own. By the same token, your personal or professional *frame of reference* may also affect your interpretation. A union representative and a management representative attempting to summarize the latest management offer would probably come up with two very different accounts. Still, we believe that in most cases it's possible to produce a reasonably objective summary of a passage if you make a conscious, good-faith effort to be unbiased and to prevent your own feelings on the subject from coloring your account of the author's text.

## USING THE SUMMARY

In some quarters, the summary has a bad reputation—and with reason. Summaries are often provided by writers as substitutes for analyses. As students, many of us have summarized books that we were supposed to *review critically*. All the same, the summary does have a place in respectable college work. First, writing a summary is an excellent way to understand what you read. This in itself is an important goal of academic study. If you don't understand your source material, chances are you won't be able to refer to it usefully in a paper. Summaries help you understand what you read because they force you to put the text into your own words. Practice with writing summaries also develops your general writing habits, since a good summary, like any other piece of good writing, is clear, coherent, and accurate.

## WHERE DO WE FIND WRITTEN SUMMARIES?

*Here are just a few of the types of writing that involve summary:*

### Academic Writing

- **Critique papers.** Summarize material in order to critique it.
- **Synthesis papers.** Summarize to show relationships between sources.
- **Analysis papers.** Summarize theoretical perspectives before applying them.
- **Research papers.** Note-taking and reporting research require summary.
- **Literature reviews.** Overviews of work presented in brief summaries.
- **Argument papers.** Summarize evidence and opposing arguments.
- **Essay exams.** Demonstrate understanding of course materials through summary.

### Workplace Writing

- **Policy briefs.** Condense complex public policy.
- **Business plans.** Summarize costs, relevant environmental impacts, and other important matters.
- **Memos, letters, and reports.** Summarize procedures, meetings, product assessments, expenditures, and more.
- **Medical charts.** Record patient data in summarized form.
- **Legal briefs.** Summarize relevant facts and arguments of cases.

Second, summaries are useful to your readers. Let's say you're writing a paper about the McCarthy era in the United States, and in part of that paper you want to discuss Arthur Miller's *The Crucible* as a dramatic treatment of the subject.

A summary of the plot would be helpful to a reader who hasn't seen or read—or who doesn't remember—the play. Or perhaps you're writing a paper about the politics of recent American military interventions. If your reader isn't likely to be familiar with American actions in Kosovo and Afghanistan, it would be a good idea to summarize these events at some early point in the paper. In many cases (an exam, for instance), you can use a summary to demonstrate your knowledge of what your professor already knows; when writing a paper, you can use a summary to inform your professor about some relatively unfamiliar source.

Third, summaries are required frequently in college-level writing. For example, on a psychology midterm, you may be asked to explain Carl Jung's theory of the collective unconscious and to show how it differs from Sigmund Freud's theory of the personal unconscious. You may have read about Jung's theory in your textbook or in a supplementary article, or your instructor may have outlined it in her lecture. You can best demonstrate your understanding of it by summarizing it. Then you'll proceed to contrast it with Freud's theory—which, of course, you must also summarize.

## THE READING PROCESS

It may seem to you that being able to tell (or retell) in summary form exactly what a passage says is a skill that ought to be taken for granted in anyone who can read at high school level. Unfortunately, this is not so: For all kinds of reasons, people don't always read carefully. In fact, it's probably safe to say that usually they don't. Either they read so inattentively that they skip over words, phrases, or even whole sentences, or, if they do see the words in front of them, they see them without registering their significance.

When a reader fails to pick up the meaning and implications of a sentence or two, usually there's no real harm done. (An exception: You could lose credit on an exam or paper because you failed to read or to realize the significance of a crucial direction by your instructor.) But over longer stretches—the paragraph, the section, the article, or the chapter—inattentive or haphazard reading interferes with your goals as a reader: to perceive the shape of the argument, to grasp the central idea, to determine the main points that compose it, to relate the parts of the whole, and to note key examples. This kind of reading takes a lot more energy and determination than casual reading. But in the long run it's an energy-saving method because it enables you to retain the content of the material and to draw upon that content in your own responses. In other words, it allows you to develop an accurate and coherent written discussion that goes beyond summary.

---

### CRITICAL READING FOR SUMMARY

- *Examine the context.* Note the credentials, occupation, and publications of the author. Identify the source in which the piece originally appeared. This information helps illuminate the author's perspective on the topic he or she is addressing.
- *Note the title and subtitle.* Some titles are straightforward, whereas the meanings of others become clearer as you read. In either case, titles typically identify the topic being addressed and often reveal the author's attitude toward that topic.
- *Identify the main point.* Whether a piece of writing contains a thesis statement in the first few paragraphs or builds its main point without stating it up front, look at the entire piece to arrive at an understanding of the overall point being made.

*(Continued on next page)*

- *Identify the subordinate points.* Notice the smaller subpoints that make up the main point, and make sure you understand how they relate to the main point. If a particular subpoint doesn't clearly relate to the main point you've identified, you may need to modify your understanding of the main point.

- *Break the reading into sections.* Notice which paragraphs make up a piece's introduction, body, and conclusion. Break up the body paragraphs into sections that address the writer's various subpoints.

- *Distinguish between points, examples, and counterarguments.* Critical reading requires careful attention to what a writer is *doing* as well as what he or she is *saying*. When a writer quotes someone else, or relays an example of something, ask yourself why this is being done. What point is the example supporting? Is another source being quoted as support for a point or as a counterargument that the writer sets out to address?

- *Watch for transitions within and between paragraphs.* In order to follow the logic of a piece of writing, as well as to distinguish between points, examples, and counterarguments, pay attention to the transitional words and phrases writers use. Transitions function like road signs, preparing the reader for what's next.

- *Read actively and recursively.* Don't treat reading as a passive, linear progression through a text. Instead, read as though you are engaged in a dialogue with the writer: Ask questions of the text as you read, make notes in the margin, underline key ideas in pencil, put question or exclamation marks next to passages that confuse or excite you. Go back to earlier points once you finish a reading, stop during your reading to recap what's come so far, and move back and forth through a text.

# HOW TO WRITE SUMMARIES

Every article you read will present its own challenge as you work to summarize it. As you'll discover, saying in a few words what has taken someone else a great many can be difficult. But like any other skill, the ability to summarize improves with practice. Here are a few pointers to get you started. They represent possible stages, or steps, in the process of writing a summary. These pointers are not meant to be ironclad rules; rather, they are designed to encourage habits of thinking that will allow you to vary your technique as the situation demands.

## GUIDELINES FOR WRITING SUMMARIES

- *Read the passage carefully.* Determine its structure. Identify the author's purpose in writing. (This will help you distinguish between more important and less important information.) Make a note in the margin when you get confused or when you think something is important; highlight or underline points sparingly, if at all.
- *Reread.* This time divide the passage into sections or stages of thought. The author's use of paragraphing will often be a useful guide. *Label,* on the passage itself, each section or stage of thought. *Underline* key ideas and terms. Write notes in the margin.
- *Write one-sentence summaries,* on a separate sheet of paper, of each stage of thought.
- *Write a thesis—a one- or two-sentence summary of the entire passage.* The thesis should express the central idea of the passage, as you have determined it from the preceding steps. You may find it useful to follow the

*(Continued on next page)*

approach of most newspaper stories—naming the *what,
who, why, where, when,* and *how* of the matter. For persuasive passages, summarize in a sentence the author's
conclusion. For descriptive passages, indicate the subject of the description and its key feature(s). Note: In
some cases, *a suitable thesis statement may already be in
the original passage.* If so, you may want to quote it
directly in your summary.

- *Write the first draft of your summary* by (1) combining
  the thesis with your list of one-sentence summaries or
  (2) combining the thesis with one-sentence summaries
  *plus* significant details from the passage. In either case,
  eliminate repetition and less important information.
  Disregard minor details or generalize them (e.g., Bill
  Clinton and George W. Bush might be generalized as
  "recent presidents"). Use as few words as possible to
  convey the main ideas.

- *Check your summary against the original passage* and
  make whatever adjustments are necessary for accuracy
  and completeness.

- *Revise your summary,* inserting transitional words
  and phrases where necessary to ensure coherence.
  Check for style. *Avoid a series of short, choppy sentences.*
  Combine sentences for a smooth, logical flow of ideas.
  Check for grammatical correctness, punctuation, and
  spelling.

## DEMONSTRATION: SUMMARY

To demonstrate these points at work, let's go through the
process of summarizing a passage of expository material—that
is, writing that is meant to inform and/or persuade. Read the
following selection carefully. Try to identify its parts and understand how they work together to create an overall statement.

## Will Your Job Be Exported?

### Alan S. Blinder

*Alan S. Blinder is the Gordon S. Rentschler Memorial Professor of Economics at Princeton University. He has served as vice chairman of the Federal Reserve Board and was a member of President Clinton's original Council of Economic Advisers.*

1    The great conservative political philosopher Edmund Burke, who probably would not have been a reader of *The American Prospect,* once observed, "You can never plan the future by the past."[1] But when it comes to preparing the American workforce for the jobs of the future, we may be doing just that.

2    For about a quarter-century, demand for labor appears to have shifted toward the college-educated and away from high-school graduates and dropouts. This shift, most economists believe, is the primary (though not the sole) reason for rising income inequality, and there is no end in sight. Economists refer to this phenomenon by an antiseptic name: skill-biased technical progress. In plain English, it means that the labor market has turned ferociously against the low skilled and the uneducated.

3    In a progressive society, such a worrisome social phenomenon might elicit some strong policy responses, such as more compensatory education, stepped-up efforts at retraining, reinforcement (rather than shredding) of the social safety net, and so on. You don't fight the market's valuation of skills; you try to mitigate its more deleterious effects. We did a bit of this in the United States in the 1990s, by raising the minimum wage and expanding the Earned Income Tax Credit.[2] Combined with tight labor

---

[1] Edmund Burke (1729–1797) was a conservative British statesman, philosopher, and author. *The American Prospect,* in which "Will Your Job Be Exported?" first appeared in the November 2006 issue, describes itself as "an authoritative magazine of liberal ideas."

[2] The Earned Income Tax Credit, an anti-poverty measure enacted by Congress in 1975 and revised in the 1980s and 1990s, provides a credit against federal income taxes for any filer who claims a dependent child.

markets, these measures improved things for the average worker. But in this decade, little or no mitigation has been attempted. Social Darwinism has come roaring back.[3]

4    With one big exception: We have expended considerable efforts to keep more young people in school longer (e.g., reducing high-school dropouts and sending more kids to college) and to improve the quality of schooling (e.g., via charter schools and No Child Left Behind[4]). Success in these domains may have been modest, but not for lack of trying. You don't have to remind Americans that education is important; the need for educational reform is etched into the public consciousness. Indeed, many people view education as the silver bullet. On hearing the question "How do we best prepare the American workforce of the future?" many Americans react reflexively with: "Get more kids to study science and math, and send more of them to college."

5    Which brings me to the future. As I argued in a recent article in *Foreign Affairs* magazine, the greatest problem for the next generation of American workers may not be lack of education, but rather "offshoring"—the movement of jobs overseas, especially to countries with much lower wages, such as India and China. Manufacturing jobs have been migrating overseas for decades. But the new wave of offshoring, of *service* jobs, is something different.

6    Traditionally, we think of service jobs as being largely immune to foreign competition. After all, you can't get your hair cut by a

---

[3] Social Darwinism, a largely discredited philosophy dating from the Victorian era and espoused by Herbert Spenser, asserts that Charles Darwin's observations on natural selection apply to human societies. Social Darwinists argue that the poor are less fit to survive than the wealthy and should, through a natural process of adaptation, be allowed to die out.

[4] Charter schools are public schools with specialized missions to operate outside of regulations that some feel restrict creativity and performance in traditional school settings. The No Child Left Behind Act of 2001 (NCLB) mandates standards-based education for all schools receiving federal funding. Both the charter schools movement and NCLB can be understood as efforts to improve public education.

barber or your broken arm set by a doctor in a distant land. But stunning advances in communication technology, plus the emergence of a vast new labor pool in Asia and Eastern Europe, are changing that picture radically, subjecting millions of presumed-safe domestic service jobs to foreign competition. And it is not necessary actually to move jobs to low-wage countries in order to restrain wage increases; the mere threat of off-shoring can put a damper on wages.

7    Service-sector offshoring is a minor phenomenon so far, Lou Dobbs notwithstanding; probably well under 1 percent of U.S. service jobs have been outsourced.[5] But I believe that service-sector offshoring will eventually exceed manufacturing-sector offshoring by a hefty margin—for three main reasons. The first is simple arithmetic: There are vastly more service jobs than manufacturing jobs in the United States (and in other rich countries). Second, the technological advances that have made service-sector offshoring possible will continue and accelerate, so the range of services that can be moved offshore will increase ineluctably. Third, the number of (e.g., Indian and Chinese) workers capable of performing service jobs offshore seems certain to grow, perhaps exponentially.

8    I do not mean to paint a bleak picture here. Ever since Adam Smith and David Ricardo, economists have explained and extolled the gains in living standards that derive from international trade.[6] Those arguments are just as valid for trade in services as for trade in goods. There really *are* net gains to the United States from expanding service-sector trade with India, China, and the rest. The offshoring problem is not about the adverse nature of what economists call the economy's eventual equilibrium. Rather, it is about

---

[5] Lou Dobbs, conservative columnist and political commentator for CNN, is well known for his anti-immigration views.

[6] Adam Smith (1723-1790), Scottish author of *An Inquiry into the Nature and Causes of the Wealth of Nations* (1776), established the foundations of modern economics. David Ricardo (1772-1823) was a British businessman, statesman, and economist who founded the classical school of economics and is best known for his studies of monetary policy.

the so-called transition—the ride from here to there. That ride, which could take a generation or more, may be bumpy. And during the long adjustment period, many U.S. wages could face downward pressure.

9    Thus far, only American manufacturing workers and a few low-end service workers (e.g., call-center operators) have been competing, at least potentially, with millions of people in faraway lands eager to work for what seems a pittance by U.S. standards. But offshoring is no longer limited to low-end service jobs. Computer code can be written overseas and e-mailed back to the United States. So can your tax return and lots of legal work, provided you do not insist on face-to-face contact with the accountant or lawyer. In writing and editing this article, I communicated with the editors and staff of *The American Prospect* only by telephone and e-mail. Why couldn't they (or I, for that matter) have been in India? The possibilities are, if not endless, at least vast.

10    What distinguishes the jobs that cannot be offshored from the ones that can? The crucial distinction is not—and this is the central point of this essay—the required levels of skill and education. These attributes have been critical to labor-market success in the past, but may be less so in the future. Instead, the new critical distinction may be that some services either require personal delivery (e.g., driving a taxi and brain surgery) or are seriously degraded when delivered electronically (e.g., college teaching—at least, I hope!), while other jobs (e.g., call centers and keyboard data entry) are not. Call the first category personal services and the second category impersonal services. With this terminology, I have three main points to make about preparing our workforce for the brave, new world of the future.

11    First, we need to think about, plan, and redesign our educational system with the crucial distinction between personal service jobs and impersonal service jobs in mind. Many of the impersonal service jobs will migrate offshore, but the personal service jobs will stay here.

12    Second, the line that divides personal services from impersonal services will move in only one direction over time, as technological progress makes it possible to deliver an ever-increasing array of services electronically.

13    Third, the novel distinction between personal and impersonal jobs is quite different from, and appears essentially unrelated to, the traditional distinction between jobs that do and do not require high levels of education.

14    For example, it is easy to offshore working in a call center, typing transcripts, writing computer code, and reading X-rays. The first two require little education; the last two require quite a lot. On the other hand, it is either impossible or very difficult to offshore janitorial services, fast-food restaurant service, college teaching, and open-heart surgery. Again, the first two occupations require little or no education, while the last two require a great deal. There seems to be little or no correlation between educational requirements (the old concern) and how "offshorable" jobs are (the new one).

15    If so, the implications could be startling. A generation from now, civil engineers (who must be physically present) may be in greater demand in the United States than computer engineers (who don't). Similarly, there might be more divorce lawyers (not offshorable) than tax lawyers (partly offshorable). More imaginatively, electricians might earn more than computer programmers. I am not predicting any of this; lots of things influence relative demands and supplies for different types of labor. But it all seems within the realm of the possible as technology continues to enhance the offshorability of even highly skilled occupations. What does seem highly likely is that the relative demand for labor in the United States will shift away from impersonal services and toward personal services, and this shift will look quite different from the familiar story of skill-biased technical progress. So Burke's warning is worth heeding.

16    I am *not* suggesting that education will become a handicap in the job market of the future. On the contrary, to the extent

that education raises productivity and that better-educated workers are more adaptable and/or more creative, a wage premium for higher education should remain. Thus, it still makes sense to send more of America's youth to college. But, over the next generation, the kind of education our young people receive may prove to be more important than how much education they receive. In that sense, a college degree may lose its exalted "silver bullet" status.

17    Looking back over the past 25 years, "stay in school longer" was excellent advice for success in the labor market. But looking forward over the next 25 years, more subtle occupational advice may be needed. "Prepare yourself for a high-end personal service occupation that is not offshorable" is a more nuanced message than "stay in school." But it may prove to be more useful. And many non-offshorable jobs—such as carpenters, electricians, and plumbers—do not require college education.

18    The hard question is how to make this more subtle advice concrete and actionable. The children entering America's educational system today, at age 5, will emerge into a very different labor market when they leave it. Given gestation periods of 13 to 17 years and more, educators and policy-makers need to be thinking now about the kinds of training and skills that will best prepare these children for their future working lives. Specifically, it is essential to educate America's youth for the jobs that will actually be available in America 20 to 30 years from now, not for the jobs that will have moved offshore.

19    Some of the personal service jobs that will remain in the United States will be very high-end (doctors), others will be less glamorous though well paid (plumbers), and some will be "dead end" (janitor). We need to think long and hard about the types of skills that best prepare people to deliver high-end personal services, and how to teach those skills in our elementary and high schools. I am not an education specialist, but it strikes me that, for example, the central thrust of No Child Left Behind is pushing the nation in exactly the wrong direction. I am all for

accountability. But the nation's school system will not build the creative, flexible, people-oriented workforce we will need in the future by drilling kids incessantly with rote preparation for standardized tests in the vain hope that they will perform as well as memory chips.

20    Starting in the elementary schools, we need to develop our youngsters' imaginations and people skills as well as thei "reading, writing, and 'rithmetic." Remember that kindergarten grade for "works and plays well with others"? It may become increasingly important in a world of personally delivered services. Such training probably needs to be continued and made more sophisticated in the secondary schools, where, for example, good communications skills need to be developed.

21    More vocational education is probably also in order. After all, nurses, carpenters, and plumbers are already scarce, and we'll likely need more of them in the future. Much vocational training now takes place in community colleges; and they, too, need to adapt their curricula to the job market of the future.

22    While it is probably still true that we should send more kids to college and increase the number who study science, math, and engineering, we need to focus on training more college students for the high-end jobs that are unlikely to move offshore, and on developing a creative workforce that will keep America incubating and developing new processes, new products, and entirely new industries. Offshoring is, after all, mostly about following and copying. American needs to lead and innovate instead, just as we have in the past.

23    Educational reform is not the whole story, of course. I suggested at the outset, for example, that we needed to repair our tattered social safety net and turn it into a retraining trampoline that bounces displaced workers back into productive employment. But many low-end personal service jobs cannot be turned into more attractive jobs simply by more training—think about janitors, fast-food workers, and nurse's aides, for example. Running a tight labor market would help such

workers, as would a higher minimum wage, an expanded Earned Income Tax Credit, universal health insurance, and the like.

24    Moving up the skill ladder, employment is concentrated in the public or quasi-public sector in a number of service occupations. Teachers and health-care workers are two prominent examples. In such cases, government policy can influence wages and working conditions directly by upgrading the structure and pay of such jobs—developing more professional early-childhood teachers and fewer casual daycare workers for example—as long as the taxpayer is willing to foot the bill. Similarly, some service jobs such as registered nurses are in short supply mainly because we are not training enough qualified personnel. Here, too, public policy can help by widening the pipeline to allow more workers through. So there are a variety of policy levers that might do some good—if we are willing to pull them.

25    But all that said, education is still the right place to start. Indeed, it is much more than that because the educational system affects the entire population and because no other institution is nearly as important when it comes to preparing our youth for the world of work. As the first industrial revolution took hold, America radically transformed (and democratized) its educational system to meet the new demands of an industrial society. We may need to do something like that again. There is a great deal at stake here. If we get this one wrong, the next generation will pay dearly. But if we get it (close to) right, the gains from trade promise coming generations a prosperous future.

26    The somewhat inchoate challenge posed here—preparing more young Americans for personal service jobs—brings to mind one of my favorite Churchill quotations: "You can always count on Americans to do the right thing—after they've tried everything else." It is time to start trying.

## Read, Reread, Highlight

Let's consider our recommended pointers for writing a summary.

As you reread the passage, note in the margins of the essay important points, shifts in thought, and questions you may have. Consider the essay's significance as a whole and its stages of thought. What does it say? How is it organized? How does each part of the passage fit into the whole? What do all these points add up to?

Here is how several paragraphs from the middle of Blinder's article might look after you have marked the main ideas by highlighting and by marginal notations.

*Offshored service jobs will eclipse lost manufacturing jobs—3 reasons*

Service-sector offshoring is a minor phenomenon so far, Lou Dobbs notwithstanding; probably well under 1 percent of U.S. service jobs have been outsourced. But I believe that service-sector offshoring will eventually exceed manufacturing-sector offshoring by a hefty margin—for three main reasons. The first is simple arithmetic: There are vastly more service jobs than manufacturing jobs in the United States (and in other rich countries). Second, the technological advances that have made service-sector offshoring possible will continue and accelerate, so the range of services that can be moved offshore will increase ineluctably. Third, the number of (e.g., Indian and Chinese) workers capable of performing service jobs offshore seems certain to grow, perhaps exponentially.

*Long-term economy will be ok. Short-to-middle term will be "bumpy"*

I do not mean to paint a bleak picture here. Ever since Adam Smith and David Ricardo, economists have explained and extolled the gains in living standards that derive from international trade. Those arguments are just as valid for trade in services as for trade in goods. There really *are* net gains to the United States from expanding service-sector trade with India, China, and the rest. The offshoring problem is not about the adverse nature of what economists call the economy's eventual equilibrium. Rather, it is about the so-called transition—the ride from here to there. That ride, which could take a generation or more, may be bumpy. And during the long adjustment period, many U.S. wages could face downward pressure.

Thus far, only American manufacturing workers and a few low-end service workers (e.g., call-center operators) have been competing, at least potentially, with millions of people in faraway lands eager to work for what seems a pittance by U.S. standards. But offshoring is no longer limited to low-end service jobs. Computer code can be written overseas and e-mailed back to the United States. So can your tax return and lots of legal work, provided you do not insist on face-to-face contact with the accountant or lawyer. In writing and editing this article, I communicated with the editors and staff of *The American Prospect* only by telephone and e-mail. Why couldn't they (or I, for that matter) have been in India? The possibilities are, if not endless, at least vast.

What distinguishes the jobs that cannot be offshored from the ones that can? The crucial distinction is not—and this is the central point of this essay—the required levels of skill and education. These attributes have been critical to labor-market success in the past, but may be less so in the future. Instead, the new critical distinction may be that some services either require personal delivery (e.g., driving a taxi and brain surgery) or are seriously degraded when delivered electronically (e.g., college teaching—at least, I hope!), while other jobs (e.g., call centers and keyboard data entry) are not. Call the first category personal services and the second category impersonal services. With this terminology, I have three main points to make about preparing our workforce for the brave, new world of the future.

First, we need to think about, plan, and redesign our educational system with the crucial distinction between

*High-end jobs to be lost*

*B's main point: Key distinction: Personal Service jobs stay; impersonal jobs go*

*3 points re: prep of future workforce*

personal service jobs and impersonal service jobs in mind. Many of the impersonal service jobs will migrate offshore, but the personal service jobs will stay here.

*Movement:*      Second, the line that divides personal services from
*impersonal*    impersonal services will move in only one direction over
→ *personal*    time, as technological progress makes it possible to deliver an ever-increasing array of services electronically.

*Level of ed.*      Third, the novel distinction between personal and
*not related to*  impersonal jobs is quite different from, and appears essen-
*future job*    tially unrelated to, the traditional distinction between jobs
*security*    that do and do not require high levels of education.

## Divide into Stages of Thought

When a selection doesn't contain sections with thematic headings, as is the case with "Will Your Job Be Exported?" how do you determine where one stage of thought ends and the next one begins? Assuming that what you have read is coherent and unified, this should not be difficult. (When a selection is unified, all of its parts pertain to the main subject; when a selection is coherent, the parts follow one another in logical order.) Look particularly for transitional sentences at the beginning of paragraphs. Such sentences generally work in one or both of two ways: (1) they summarize what has come before; (2) they set the stage for what is to follow.

Look at the sentences that open paragraphs 5 and 10: "Which brings me to the future" and "What distinguishes the jobs that cannot be offshored from the ones that can?" In both cases Blinder makes a clear announcement. Grammatically speaking, "Which brings me to the future" is a fragment, not a sentence. Experienced writers will use fragments on occasion to good effect, as in this case. The fragment clearly has the sense of a complete thought: the pronoun "which" refers readers to the content of the preceding paragraphs, asking readers to summarize that content and then, with the predicate "brings me to the future," to move forward into the next part of the article. Similarly, the question "What distinguishes the jobs that cannot be offshored from the ones that can?" implicitly asks readers to recall an important distinction just made (the definitions of offshorable and non-offshorable jobs) and then clearly moves readers forward to new, related content. As you can see, the openings of paragraphs 5 and 10 announce new sections in the article.

Each section of an article generally takes several paragraphs to develop. Between paragraphs, and almost certainly between sections of an article, you will usually find transitions that help you understand what you have just read and what you are about to read. For articles that have no subheadings, try writing your own section headings in the margins as you take notes. Blinder's article can be divided into five sections.

*Section 1: Recent past: education of workers important*—For twenty-five years, the labor market has rewarded workers with higher levels of education (paragraphs 1–4).

*Section 2: Future: ed level won't always matter—workers in service sector will lose jobs offshore*—Once thought immune to outsourcing, even highly trained service workers will lose jobs to overseas competition (paragraphs 5–9).

*Section 3: Which service jobs at highest risk?*—<u>Personal</u> service workers are safe; <u>impersonal</u> service workers, both highly educated and not, will see jobs offshored (paragraphs 10–15).

*Section 4: Educating the future workforce*—Emphasizing the <u>kind</u>, not amount, of education will help to prepare workers for jobs of the future (paragraphs 16–22).

*Section 5: Needed policy reforms*—Government can improve conditions for low-end service workers and expand opportunities for higher-end service workers; start with education (paragraphs 23–26).

## Write a Brief Summary of Each Stage of Thought

The purpose of this step is to wean you from the language of the original passage, so that you are not tied to it when writing the summary. Here are brief summaries, one for each stage of thought in "Will Your Job Be Exported?"

*Section 1:* Recent past: education of workers important (paragraphs 1–4).

> For the past twenty-five years, the greater a worker's skill or level of education, the better and more stable the job.

*Section 2:* Future: ed level won't always matter—workers in service sector will lose jobs offshore (paragraphs 5–9).

> Advances in technology have brought to the service sector the same pressures that forced so many manufacturing jobs offshore to China and India. The rate of offshoring in the service sector will accelerate and "eventually exceed" job losses in manufacturing, says Blinder, and jobs requiring both relatively little education (like call-center staffing) and extensive education (like software development) will be lost to workers overseas.

*Section 3:* Which service jobs at highest risk? (paragraphs 10–15).

> While "personal services" workers (like barbers and sur-geons) will be relatively safe from offshoring because their work requires close physical proximity to customers, "imper-sonal services" workers (like call-center operators and radiol-ogists), regardless of their skill or education, will be at risk because their work can be completed remotely without loss of quality and then delivered via phone or computer. Blinder believes that "the relative demand for labor in the United States will [probably] shift away from impersonal services and toward personal services."

*Section 4*: Educating the future workforce (paragraphs 16–22).

Blinder advises young people to plan for "a high-end personal service occupation that is not offshorable." He also urges educators to prepare the future workforce by anticipating the needs of a personal services economy and redesigning classroom instruction and vocational training accordingly.

*Section 5*: Needed policy reforms (paragraphs 23–26).

Blinder urges the government to develop policies that will improve wages and conditions for low-wage personal service workers (like janitors); to encourage more low-wage workers (like daycare providers) to retrain and take on better jobs; and to increase opportunities for professional and vocational training in high-demand areas (like nursing and carpentry).

## Write a Thesis: A Brief Summary of the Entire Passage

The thesis is the most general statement of a summary (or any other type of academic writing). It is the statement that announces the paper's subject and the claim that you or—in the case of a summary—another author will be making about that subject. Every paragraph of a paper illuminates the thesis by providing supporting detail or explanation. The relationship of these paragraphs to the thesis is analogous to the relationship of the sentences within a paragraph to the topic sentence. Both the thesis and the topic sentences are general statements (the thesis being the more general) that are followed by systematically arranged details.

To ensure clarity for the reader, *the first sentence of your summary should begin with the author's thesis, regardless of where it appears in the article itself.* An author may locate her thesis at the beginning of her work, in which case the thesis operates as a general principle from which details of the presentation follow. This is called a *deductive* organization: thesis first, supporting details second. Alternatively, an author may locate his thesis at the end of the work, in which case the author begins with specific details and builds toward a more general conclusion, or thesis. This is called an *inductive* organization. And, as you might expect, an author might locate the thesis anywhere between beginning and end, at whatever point it seems best positioned.*

A thesis consists of a subject and an assertion about that subject. How can we go about fashioning an adequate thesis for a summary of Blinder's article? Probably no two versions of Blinder's thesis statement would be worded identically, but it is fair to say that any reasonable thesis will indicate that Blinder's subject is the future loss to off-shoring of American jobs in the service sector—that part of the economy that delivers services to consumers, from low end (e.g., janitorial services) to high end (e.g., neurosurgery). How does Blinder view the situation? How secure will service jobs be if Blinder's distinction between personal and impersonal services is valid? Looking back over our section summaries, we find that Blinder insists on three points: (1) that education and skill matter less than they once did in determining job quality and security; (2) that the distinction between personal and impersonal services will increasingly

---

* Blinder positions his thesis midway through his five-section article. He opens the selection by discussing the role of education in the labor market during the past twenty-five years (Section 1, pars. 1–4). He continues by summarizing an earlier article on the ways in which service jobs are following manufacturing jobs offshore (Section 2, pars. 5–9). He then presents a two-sentence thesis in answer to the question that opens paragraph 10: "What distinguishes the jobs that cannot be offshored from the ones that can?" The remainder of the article either develops this thesis (Section 3, pars. 10–15) or follows its implications for education (Section 4, pars. 16–22) and public policy (Section 5, pars. 23–26).

determine which jobs remain and which are offshored; and (3) that the distinction between personal and impersonal has implications for both the future of education and public policy.

Does Blinder make a statement anywhere in this passage that pulls all this together? Examine paragraph 10 and you will find his thesis—two sentences that answer his question about which jobs will and will not be sent offshore: "The crucial distinction is not—and this is the central point of this essay—the required levels of skill and education. . . . Instead, the new critical distinction may be that some services either require personal delivery (e.g., driving a taxi and brain surgery) or are seriously degraded when delivered electronically (e.g., college teaching—at least, I hope!), while other jobs (e.g., call centers and keyboard data entry) are not."

You may have learned that a thesis statement must be expressed in a single sentence. We would offer a slight rewording of this generally sound advice and say that a thesis statement must be *expressible* in a single sentence. For reasons of emphasis or style, a writer might choose to distribute a thesis across two or more sentences. Certainly, the sense of Blinder's thesis can take the form of a single statement: "The critical distinction is X, not Y." For reasons largely of emphasis, he divides his thesis into two sentences—in fact, separating these sentences with another sentence that explains the first part of the thesis: "These attributes [that is, skill and education] have been critical to labor-market success in the past, but may be less so in the future."

Here is a one-sentence version of Blinder's two-sentence thesis:

> The quality and security of future jobs in America's service sector will be determined by how "offshorable" those jobs are.

Notice that the statement anticipates a summary of the *entire* article: both the discussion leading up to Blinder's thesis and his discussion after. To clarify for our readers the fact that this idea is Blinder's and not ours, we might qualify the thesis as follows:

> In "Will Your Job Be Exported?" economist Alan S. Blinder argues that the quality and security of future jobs in America's service sector will be determined by how "offshorable" those jobs are.

The first sentence of a summary is crucially important, for it orients readers by letting them know what to expect in the coming paragraphs. In the example above, the first sentence refers directly to an article, its author, and the thesis for the upcoming summary. The author and title reference also could be indicated in the summary's title (if this were a free-standing summary), in which case their mention could be dropped from the thesis statement. And lest you become frustrated too quickly with how much effort it takes to come up with this crucial sentence, keep in mind that writing an acceptable thesis for a summary takes time. In this case, it took three drafts, roughly ten minutes, to compose a thesis and another few minutes of fine-tuning after a draft of the entire summary was completed. The thesis needed revision because the first draft was vague; the second draft was improved but too specific on a secondary point; the third draft was more complete but too general on a key point:

> *Draft 1:*  We must begin now to train young people for high-quality personal service jobs.
> *(Vague. The question of why we should begin training isn't clear, nor is the phrase "high-quality personal service jobs." Define this term or make it more general.)*

> *Draft 2:*  Alan S. Blinder argues that unlike in the past, the quality and security of future American jobs will not be determined by skill level or education but rather by how "offshorable" those jobs are.
> *(Better, but the reference to "skill level or education" is secondary to Blinder's main point about offshorable jobs.)*

*Draft 3*: In "Will Your Job Be Exported?" economist Alan S. Blinder argues that the quality and security of future jobs will be determined by how "offshorable" those jobs are.

*(Close—but not "all" jobs. Blinder specifies which types of jobs are "offshorable.")*

*Final Draft*: In "Will Your Job Be Exported?" economist Alan S. Blinder argues that the quality and security of future jobs in America's service sector will be determined by how "offshorable" those jobs are.

## Write the First Draft of the Summary

Let's consider two possible summaries of Blinder's article: (1) a short summary, combining a thesis with brief section summaries, and (2) a longer summary, combining thesis, brief section summaries, and some carefully chosen details. Again, keep in mind that you are reading final versions; each of the following summaries is the result of at least two full drafts. Highlighting indicates transitions added to smooth the flow of the summary.

### Summary 1: Combine Thesis Sentence with Brief Section Summaries

In "Will Your Job Be Exported?" economist Alan S. Blinder argues that the quality and security of future jobs in America's service sector will be determined by how "offshorable" those jobs are. For the past twenty-five years, the greater a worker's skill or level of education, the better and more stable the job. No longer. Advances in technology have brought to the service sector the same pressures that forced so many manufacturing jobs offshore to China and India. The rate of offshoring in the service sector will accelerate, and jobs requiring both relatively little education (like call-center staffing) and extensive education (like software development) will increasingly be lost to workers overseas.

These losses will "eventually exceed" losses in manufacturing, but not all services jobs are equally at risk. While "personal services" workers (like barbers and surgeons) will be relatively safe from offshoring because their work requires close physical proximity to customers, "impersonal services" workers (like call-center operators and radiologists), regardless of their skill or education, will be at risk because their work can be completed remotely without loss of quality and then delivered via phone or computer. "[T]he relative demand for labor in the United States will [probably] shift away from impersonal services and toward personal services."

Blinder recommends three courses of action: He advises young people to plan for "a high-end personal service occupation that is not offshorable." He urges educators to prepare the future workforce by anticipating the needs of a personal services economy and redesigning classroom instruction and vocational training accordingly. Finally, he urges the government to adopt policies that will improve existing personal services jobs by increasing wages for low-wage workers; retraining workers to take on better jobs; and increasing opportunities in high-demand, well-paid areas like nursing and carpentry. Ultimately, Blinder wants America to prepare a new generation to "lead and innovate" in an economy that will continue exporting jobs that require "following and copying."

## The Strategy of the Shorter Summary

This short summary consists essentially of a restatement of Blinder's thesis plus the section summaries, modified or expanded a little for stylistic purposes. You'll recall that Blinder locates his thesis midway through the article, in paragraph 10. But note that this model summary *begins* with a restatement of his thesis. Notice also the relative weight given to the section summaries within the model. Blinder's main point, his "critical distinction" between personal and impersonal services jobs, is summarized in paragraph 2 of the model. The other paragraphs combine summaries of relatively less important (that is, supporting or explanatory) material. Paragraph 1 combines summaries of the article's Sections 1 and 2; paragraph 3 combines summaries of Sections 4 and 5.

Between the thesis and the section summaries, notice the insertion of three (highlighted) transitions. The first—a fragment (*No longer*)—bridges the first paragraph's summaries of Sections 1 and 2 of Blinder's article. The second transition links a point Blinder makes in his Section 2 (*Losses in the service sector will "eventually exceed" losses in manufacturing*) with an introduction to the key point he will make in Section 3 (*Not all service jobs are equally at risk*). The third transition (*Blinder recommends three courses of action*) bridges the summary of Blinder's Section 3 to summaries of Sections 4 and 5. Each transition, then, links sections of the whole: each casts the reader back to recall points just made; each casts the reader forward by announcing related points about to be made. Our model ends with a summary of Blinder's motivation for writing, the sense of which is implied by the section summaries but nowhere made explicit.

### Summary 2: Combine Thesis Sentence, Section Summaries, and Carefully Chosen Details

The thesis and brief section summaries could also be used as the outline for a more detailed summary. However, most of the details in the passage won't be necessary in a summary. It isn't necessary even in a longer summary of this passage to discuss all of Blinder's examples of jobs that are more or less likely to be sent offshore. It would be appropriate, though, to mention one example of such a job; to review his reasons for thinking "that service-sector offshoring will eventually exceed manufacturing-sector offshoring by a hefty margin"; and to expand on his point that a college education in itself will no longer ensure job security.

None of these details appeared in the first summary; but in a longer summary, a few carefully selected details might be desirable for clarity. How do you decide which details to include? First, working with Blinder's point that one's job type (personal services vs. impersonal services) will matter more for future job quality and security than did the once highly regarded "silver bullet" of education, you may want to cite some of the most persuasive evidence supporting this idea. For example, you could explore why some highly paid physicians, like radiologists, might find themselves competing for jobs with lower-paid physicians overseas. Further, your expanded summary might reflect the relative weight Blinder gives to education (seven paragraphs, the longest of the article's five sections).

You won't always know which details to include and which to exclude. Developing good judgment in comprehending and summarizing texts is largely a matter of reading skill and prior knowledge (see page 2). Consider the analogy of the seasoned mechanic who can pinpoint an engine problem by simply listening to a characteristic sound that to a less-experienced person is just noise. Or consider the chess player who can plot three separate winning strategies from a board position that to a novice looks like a hopeless jumble. In the same way, the more practiced a reader you are, the more knowledgeable you become about the subject and the better able you will be to make critical distinctions between elements of greater and lesser importance. In the meantime, read as carefully as you can and use your own best judgment as to how to present your material.

Here's one version of a completed summary with carefully chosen details. Note that we have highlighted phrases and sentences added to the original, briefer summary.

In "Will Your Job Be Exported?" economist Alan S. Blinder argues that the quality and security of future jobs in America's service sector will be determined by how "offshorable" those jobs are. For the past twenty-five years, the greater a worker's skill or level of education, the better and more stable the job. Americans have long regarded education as the "silver bullet" that could propel motivated people to better jobs and a better life. No longer. Advances in technology have brought to the service sector the same pressures that forced so many manufacturing jobs offshore to China and India. The rate of offshoring in the service sector will accelerate, says Blinder, and jobs requiring both relatively little education (like call-center staffing) and extensive education (like software development) will increasingly be lost to workers overseas.

Blinder expects that job losses in the service sector will "eventually exceed" losses in manufacturing, for three reasons. Developed countries have more service jobs than manufacturing jobs; as technology speeds communications, more service jobs will be offshorable; and the numbers of qualified offshore workers is increasing. Service jobs lost to foreign competition may cause a "bumpy" period as the global economy sorts out what work gets done where, by whom. In time, as the global economy finds its "eventual equilibrium," offshoring will benefit the United States; but the consequences in the meantime may be painful for many.

That pain will not be shared equally by all service workers, however. While "personal service" workers (like barbers and surgeons) will be relatively safe from offshoring because their work requires close physical proximity to customers, "impersonal service" workers (like audio transcribers and radiologists), regardless of their skill or education, will be at risk because their work can be completed remotely without loss of quality and then delivered via phone or computer. In the coming decades, says Blinder, "the relative demand for labor in the United States will [probably] shift away from impersonal services and toward personal services." This shift will be influenced by the desire to keep good jobs in the United States while exporting jobs that require "following and copying." Highly trained computer coders will face the same pressures of outsourcing as relatively untrained call-center attendants. A tax attorney whose work requires no face-to-face interaction with clients may see her work migrate overseas while a divorce attorney, who must interact with clients on a case-by-case basis, may face no such competition. Same educations, different outcomes: what determines their fates in a global economy is the nature of their work (that is, personal vs. impersonal), not their level of education.

Based on this analysis, Blinder recommends three courses of action: First, he advises young people to plan for "a high-end personal service occupation that is not offshorable." Many good jobs, like carpentry and plumbing, will not require a college degree. Next, Blinder urges educators to prepare the future workforce by anticipating the needs of a personal services economy and redesigning classroom instruction and vocational training accordingly. These efforts should begin in elementary school and develop imagination and interpersonal skills rather than capacities for rote memorization. Finally, Blinder urges the government to develop policies that will improve wages and conditions for low-wage personal services workers (like janitors); to encourage more low-wage workers (like daycare providers) to retrain and take on better service jobs; and to increase opportunities for professional and vocational training for workers in high-demand services areas (like nurses and electricians). Ultimately, Blinder wants America to prepare a new generation of workers who will "lead and innovate . . . just as we have in the past."

## The Strategy of the Longer Summary

Compared to the first, briefer summary, this effort (seventy percent longer than the first) includes Blinder's reasons for suggesting that job losses in the services sector will exceed losses in manufacturing. It emphasizes Blinder's point that job type (personal vs. impersonal services), not a worker's education level, will ensure job security. It includes Blinder's point that offshoring in the service sector is part of a larger global economy seeking "equilibrium." And it offers more on Blinder's thoughts concerning the education of future workers.

The final two of our suggested steps for writing summaries are (1) to check your summary against the original passage, making sure that you have included all the important ideas, and (2) to revise so that the summary reads smoothly and coherently. The structure of this summary generally reflects the structure of the original article—with one significant departure, as noted earlier. Blinder uses a modified inductive approach, stating his thesis midway through the article. The summary, however, states the thesis immediately, then proceeds deductively to develop that thesis.

## HOW LONG SHOULD A SUMMARY BE?

The length of a summary depends both on the length of the original passage and on the use to which the summary will be put. If you are summarizing an entire article, a good rule of thumb is that your summary should be no longer than one-fourth the length of the original passage. Of course, if you were summarizing an entire chapter or even an entire book, it would have to be much shorter than that. The longer summary above is one-quarter the length of Alan Blinder's original. Although it shouldn't be very much longer, you have seen (p. 26) that it could be quite a bit shorter.

The length as well as the content of the summary also depends on the *purpose* to which it will be put. Let's suppose you decided to use Blinder's piece in a paper that dealt with the loss of manufacturing jobs in the United States and the rise of the service economy. In this case, in an effort to explain the complexities of the service economy to your readers, you might summarize *only* Blinder's core distinction between jobs in personal services and impersonal services, likely mentioning that jobs in the latter category are at risk of offshoring. If, instead, you were writing a paper in which you argued that the forces of globalization will eventually collapse the world's economies into a single, global economy, you would likely give less attention to Blinder's distinction between personal and impersonal services. More to the point might be his observation that highly skilled, highly educated workers in the United States are now finding themselves competing with qualified, lower-wage workers in China and India. Thus, depending on your purpose, you would summarize either selected portions of a source or an entire source. We will see this process more fully demonstrated in the upcoming chapters on syntheses.

## AVOIDING PLAGIARISM

Plagiarism is generally defined as the attempt to pass off the work of another as one's own. Whether born out of calculation or desperation, plagiarism is the least tolerated offense in the academic world. The fact that most plagiarism is unintentional—arising from ignorance of conventions rather than deceitfulness—makes no difference to many professors.

The ease of cutting and pasting whole blocks of text from Web sources into one's own paper makes it tempting for some to take the easy way out and avoid doing their own research and writing. But apart from the serious ethical issues involved, the same technology that makes such acts possible also makes it possible for instructors to detect them. Software marketed to instructors allows them to conduct Web searches, using suspicious phrases as keywords. The results often provide irrefutable evidence of plagiarism.

Of course, plagiarism is not confined to students. Recent years have seen a number of high-profile cases—some of them reaching the front pages of newspapers—of well-known scholars who were shown to have copied passages from sources into their own book manuscripts, without proper attribution. In some cases, the scholars maintained that these appropriations were simply a matter of carelessness, that in the press and volume of work they had lost track of which words were theirs and which were the words of their sources. But such excuses sounded hollow: These careless acts inevitably embarrassed the scholars professionally, tarnished their otherwise fine work and reputations, and disappointed their many admirers.

You can avoid plagiarism and charges of plagiarism by following the basic rules provided on page 36.

Following is a passage of text, along with several student versions of the ideas represented. (The passage is from Richard Rovere's article on Senator Joseph P. McCarthy, "The Most Gifted and Successful Demagogue This Country Has Ever Known.")

> McCarthy never seemed to believe in himself or in anything he had said. He knew that Communists were not in charge of American foreign policy. He knew that they weren't running the United States Army. He knew that he had spent five years looking for Communists in the government and that—although some must certainly have been there, since Communists had turned up in practically every other major government in the world—he hadn't come up with even one.*

One student wrote the following version of this passage:

> McCarthy never believed in himself or in anything he had said. He knew that Communists were not in charge of American foreign

---

* Richard Rovere, "The Most Gifted and Successful Demagogue This Country Has Ever Known," *New York Times Magazine,* April 30, 1967.

policy and weren't running the United States Army. He knew that he had spent five years looking for Communists in the government, and although there must certainly have been some there, since Communists were in practically every other major government in the world, he hadn't come up with even one.

Clearly, this is intentional plagiarism. The student has copied the original passage almost word for word.

Here is another version of the same passage:

McCarthy knew that Communists were not running foreign policy or the Army. He also knew that although there must have been some Communists in the government, he hadn't found a single one, even though he had spent five years looking.

This student has attempted to put the ideas into her own words, but both the wording and the sentence structure are so heavily dependent on the original passage that even if it *were* cited, most professors would consider it plagiarism.

In the following version, the student has sufficiently changed the wording and sentence structure, and she uses a *signal phrase* (a phrase used to introduce a quotation or paraphrase, signaling to the reader that the words to follow come from someone else) to properly credit the information to Rovere, so that there is no question of plagiarism:

According to Richard Rovere, McCarthy was fully aware that Communists were running neither the government nor the Army. He also knew that he hadn't found a single Communist in government, even after a lengthy search (192).

And although this is not a matter of plagiarism, as noted above, it's essential to quote accurately. You are not permitted to change any part of a quotation or to omit any part of it without using brackets or ellipses.

## RULES FOR AVOIDING PLAGIARISM

- Cite *all* quoted material and *all* summarized and para-phrased material, unless the information is common knowledge (e.g., the Civil War was fought from 1861 to 1865).
- Make sure that both the *wording* and the *sentence structure* of your summaries and paraphrases are substantially your own.

# 2

# Critical Reading
## and Critique

## CRITICAL READING

When writing papers in college, you are often called
on to respond critically to source materials. Critical reading requires the abilities to both summarize and evaluate
a presentation. As you have seen in Chapter 1, a *summary*
is a brief restatement in your own words of the
content of a passage. An *evaluation*, however, is more
ambitious.

In your college work, you read to gain and *use* new information; but because sources are not equally valid or equally
useful, you must learn to distinguish critically among them
by evaluating them.

There is no ready-made formula for determining
validity. Critical reading and its written equivalent—the
*critique*—require discernment, sensitivity, imagination,
knowledge of the subject, and above all, willingness to
become involved in what you read. These skills cannot
be taken for granted and are developed only through repeat-
ed practice. You must begin somewhere, though, and
we recommend that you start by posing two broad
categories of questions about passages, articles, and books
that you read: (1) To what extent does the author succeed
in his or her purpose? (2) To what extent do you agree with
the author?

## Question 1: To What Extent Does the Author Succeed in His or Her Purpose?

All critical reading *begins with an accurate summary.* Thus, before attempting an evaluation, you must be able to locate an author's thesis and identify the selection's content and structure. You must understand the author's *purpose.* Authors write to inform, to persuade, and to entertain. A given piece may be primarily *informative* (a summary of the research on cloning), primarily *persuasive* (an argument on why the government must do something to alleviate homelessness), or primarily *entertaining* (a play about the frustrations of young lovers). Or it may be all three (as in John Steinbeck's novel *The Grapes of Wrath,* about migrant

---

### WHERE DO WE FIND WRITTEN CRITIQUES?

*Here are just a few types of writing that involve critique:*

#### Academic Writing

- **Research papers.** Critique sources in order to establish their usefulness.
- **Position papers.** Stake out a position by critiquing other positions.
- **Book reviews.** Combine summary with critique.
- **Essay exams.** Demonstrate understanding of course material by critiquing it.

#### Workplace Writing

- **Legal briefs and legal arguments.** Critique previous arguments made by opposing counsel.
- **Business plans and proposals.** Critique other less cost-effective, efficient, or reasonable approaches.
- **Policy briefs.** Communicate failings of policies and legislation through critique.

workers during the Great Depression). Sometimes, authors are not fully conscious of their purpose. Sometimes their purpose changes as they write. Also, multiple purposes can overlap: An essay may need to inform the reader about an issue in order to make a persuasive point. But if the finished piece is coherent, it will have a primary reason for having been written, and it should be apparent that the author is attempting primarily to inform, persuade, or entertain a particular audience. To identify this primary reason—this purpose—is your first job as a critical reader. Your next job is to determine how successful the author has been.

As a critical reader, you bring various criteria, or standards of judgment, to bear when you read pieces intended to inform, persuade, or entertain.

## Writing to Inform

A piece intended to inform will provide definitions, describe or report on a process, recount a story, give historical background, and/or provide facts and figures. An informational piece responds to questions such as these:

What (or who) is _____?

How does _____ work?

What is the controversy or problem about?

What happened?

How and why did it happen?

What were the results?

What are the arguments for and against _____?

To the extent that an author answers these and related questions and the answers are a matter of verifiable record (you could check for accuracy if you had the time and inclination), the selection is intended to inform. Having determined this, you can organize your response by considering three other criteria: accuracy, significance, and fair interpretation of information.

*Evaluating Informative Writing*

**Accuracy of Information.** If you are going to use any of the information presented, you must be satisfied that it is trustworthy. One of your responsibilities as a critical reader, then, is to find out if it is accurate. This means you should check facts against other sources. Government publications are often good resources for verifying facts about political legislation, population data, crime statistics, and the like. You can also search key terms in library databases and on the Web. Since material on the Web is essentially self-published, however, you must be especially vigilant in assessing its legitimacy. A wealth of useful information is now available on the Internet—but there is also a tremendous amount of misinformation, distorted "facts," and unsupported opinion.

**Significance of Information.** One useful question that you can put to a reading is "So what?" In the case of selections that attempt to inform, you may reasonably wonder whether the information makes a difference. What can the reader gain from this information? How is knowledge advanced by the publication of this material? Is the information of importance to you or to others in a particular audience? Why or why not?

**Fair Interpretation of Information.** At times you will read reports, the sole purpose of which is to relate raw data or information. In these cases, you will build your response on Question 1, introduced on page 38: To what extent does the author succeed in his or her purpose? More frequently, once an author has presented information, he or she will attempt to evaluate or interpret it—which is only reasonable, since information that has not been evaluated or interpreted is of little use. One of your tasks as a critical reader is to make a distinction between the author's presentation of facts and figures and his or her attempts to evaluate them. Watch for shifts from straightforward descriptions of factual information ("20 percent of the population") to assertions about what this information means ("a *mere* 20 percent of the population"), what its implications are, and so on. Pay attention to whether the logic with which the author connects interpretation with facts is sound. You may find that the information is valuable but the interpretation is not. Perhaps the author's conclusions are not justified. Could you offer a contrary explanation for the same facts? Does more information need to be gathered before firm conclusions can be drawn? Why?

## Writing to Persuade

Writing is frequently intended to persuade—that is, to influence the reader's thinking. To make a persuasive case, the writer must begin with an assertion that is arguable, some statement about which reasonable people could disagree. Such an assertion, when it serves as the essential organizing principle of the article or book, is called a *thesis*. Here are two examples:

> Because they do not speak English, many children in this affluent land are being denied their fundamental right to equal educational opportunity.

> Bilingual education, which has been stridently promoted by a small group of activists with their own agenda, is detrimental to the very students it is supposed to serve.

Thesis statements such as these—and the subsequent assertions used to help support them—represent conclusions that authors have drawn as a result of researching and thinking about an issue. You go through the same process yourself when you write persuasive papers or critiques. And just as you are entitled to evaluate critically the assertions of authors you read, so your professors—and other students—are entitled to evaluate *your* assertions, whether they be written arguments or comments made in class discussion.

Keep in mind that writers organize arguments by arranging evidence to support one conclusion and oppose (or dismiss) another. You can assess the validity of an argument and its conclusion by determining whether the author has (1) clearly defined key terms, (2) used information fairly, and (3) argued logically and not fallaciously (see pages 44–53).

### Evaluating Persuasive Writing

Read the argument that follows on the nation's troubled "star" system for producing elite athletes and dancers. We will illustrate our discussion on defining terms, using information fairly, and arguing logically by referring to Joan Ryan's argument. The example critique that follows these illustrations will be based on this same argument.

---

### We Are Not Created Equal in Every Way

#### Joan Ryan

*In an opinion piece for* The San Francisco Chronicle *(December 12, 2000), columnist and reporter Joan Ryan takes a stand on whether the San Francisco Ballet School did or did not discriminate against 8-year-old Fredrika Keefer when it declined to admit her on the grounds that she had the wrong body type to be a successful ballerina. Keefer's mother subsequently sued the ballet school for discrimination, claiming that the rejection had caused her daughter confusion and humiliation. Ryan examines the question of setting admissions standards and also the problems some parents create by pushing their young children to meet these standards.*

1    Fredrika Keefer is an 8-year-old girl who likes to dance, just like her mother and grandmother before her. She relishes playing the lead role of Clara in the Pacific Dance Theater's "Petite Nutcracker." So perhaps she is not as shy as many fourth-graders. But I wonder how she feels about her body being a topic of public discussion.

2     Fredrika and her mother filed suit because, as her mother puts it, she "did not have the right body type to be accepted" by the San Francisco Ballet School. "My daughter is very sophisticated, so she understands why we're doing this," Krissy Keefer said. "And the other kids think she's a celebrity."

3     There is no question Keefer raises a powerful point in her complaint. The values placed on an unnaturally thin body for female performers drives some dancers to potentially fatal eating disorders. But that isn't exactly the issue here. This is: Does the San Francisco Ballet School have the right to give preference to leaner body types in selecting 300 students from this year's 1,400 applicants?

4     Yes, for the same reason UC Berkeley can reject students based on mental prowess and a fashion modeling school can reject students based on comeliness. Every institution has standards that weed out those who are less likely to succeed. I know this flies in the face of American ideals. But the reality is that all men and women are not created equal.

5     Like it or not, the ethereal, elongated body that can float on air is part of the look and feel of classical ballet. You and I might think ballet would be just as pleasing with larger bodies. But most of those who practice the art disagree, which is their right. This doesn't mean that women with different body types cannot become professional dancers. They just have to find a different type of dance—jazz, tap, modern—just as athletes have to find sports that fit certain body types. A tall, blocky man, for example, could not be a jockey but he could play baseball.

6     Having written extensively about the damaging pressures on young female gymnasts and figure skaters, I understand Keefer's concerns about body type. But for me, the more disturbing issue in this story isn't about weight but age.

7     The San Francisco Ballet School is very clear and open about the fact it is strictly a training ground for professional dancers. "We are not a recreation department," said a ballet spokeswoman.

8     In other words, children at age 8 are already training for adult careers. By age 12 or 13, the children are training so much that they either begin homeschooling or attend a school that accommodates

the training schedule. The child has thrown all her eggs into this one little basket at an age when most kids can barely decide what to wear to school in the morning. And the child knows the parents are paying lots of money for this great opportunity.

9    The ballet school usually has a psychologist to counsel the students, but at the moment there is not one on staff. And the parents are given no training by the school on the pitfalls their daughters might encounter as they climb the ballet ladder: weight issues, physical ailments, social isolation, psychological pressure.

10    Just as in elite gymnastics and figure skating, these children are in the netherland of the law. They are neither hobbyists nor professionals. There is no safety net for them, no arm of government that makes sure that the adults in their lives watch out for their best interests.

11    Keefer said she would drop her lawsuit if the school accepted her daughter. The San Francisco Ballet School offers the best training in the Bay Area, she said. Fredrika, however, has said she is quite happy dancing where she is. Still, the mother gets to decide what's best for her daughter's dancing career. The child is clearly too young to make such a decision. Yet, in the skewed logic of elite athletics and dancing, she is not too young to pay the price for it.

---

*Persuasive Strategies*

**Clearly Defined Terms.** The validity of an argument depends to some degree on how carefully an author has defined key terms. Take the assertion, for example, that American society must be grounded in "family values." Just what do people who use this phrase mean by it? The validity of their argument depends on whether they and their readers agree on a definition of "family values"—as well as what it means to be "grounded in" family values. If an author writes that in the recent past "America's elites accepted as a matter of course that a free society can sustain itself only through virtue and temperance in the people" (Charles

Murray, "The Coming White Underclass," *Wall Street Journal*, October 20, 1993), readers need to know what exactly the author means by "elites" and by "virtue and temperance" before they can assess the validity of the argument. In such cases, the success of the argument—its ability to persuade—hinges on the definition of a term. So, in responding to an argument, be sure you (and the author) are clear on what exactly is being argued. Unless you are, no informed response is possible.

Ryan uses several terms important for understanding her argument. The primary one is the "body type" that the San Francisco Ballet School uses as an application standard. Ryan defines this type (paragraph 5) as "the elongated body that can float on air." Leaving other terms undefined, she writes that the ballet school's use of body type as a standard "flies in the face of American ideals" (paragraph 4). Exactly *which* ideals she leaves for the reader to define: They might include fair play, equality of access, or the belief that decisions ought to be based on talent, not appearance. The reader cannot be sure. When she reports that a spokeswoman for the school stated that "We are not a recreation department," Ryan assumes the reader will understand the reference. The mission of a recreation department is to give *all* participants equal access. In a youth recreation league, children of all abilities would get to play in a baseball game. In a league for elite athletes, in which winning was a priority, coaches would permit only the most talented children to play.

When writing a paper, you will need to decide, like Ryan, which terms to define and which you can assume the reader will define in the same way you do. As the writer of a critique, you should identify and discuss any undefined or ambiguous term that might give rise to confusion.

**Fair Use of Information**. Information is used as evidence in support of arguments. When you encounter such evidence, ask yourself two questions: (1) "Is the information accurate and up to date?" At least a portion of an argument becomes invalid when the information used to support it is inaccurate or out of date. (2) "Has the author cited *representative* information?" The evidence used in an argument must be presented in a spirit of fair play. An author is less than ethical when he presents only evidence favoring his own views even though he is well aware that contrary evidence exists. For instance, it would be dishonest to argue that an economic recession is imminent and to cite only indicators of economic downturn while ignoring and failing to cite contrary (positive) evidence.

As you have seen, "We Are Not Created Equal in Every Way" is not an information-heavy essay. The success of the piece turns on the author's use of logic, not facts and figures. In this case, the reader has every reason to trust that Ryan has presented the facts accurately: An 8-year-old girl has been denied admission to a prestigious ballet school. The mother of the girl has sued the school.

### Logical Argumentation: Avoiding Logical Fallacies

At some point, you will need to respond to the logic of the argument itself. To be convincing, an argument should be governed by principles of *logic*—clear and orderly thinking. This does *not* mean that an argument should not be biased. A biased argument—that is, an argument weighted toward one point of view and against others, which is in fact the nature of argument—may be valid as long as it is logically sound.

Several examples of faulty thinking and logical fallacies to watch for follow.

**Emotionally Loaded Terms**. Writers sometimes attempt to sway readers by using emotionally charged words. Words with positive connotations (e.g., "family values") are intended to sway readers to the author's point of view; words with negative connotations (e.g., "paying the price") try to sway readers away from an opposing point of view. The fact that an author uses emotionally loaded terms does not necessarily invalidate an argument. Emotional appeals are perfectly legitimate and time-honored modes of persuasion. But in academic writing, which is grounded in logical argumentation, they should not be the *only* means of persuasion. You should be sensitive to *how* emotionally loaded terms are being used. In particular, are they being used deceptively or to hide the essential facts?

Ryan appeals to our desire to protect children in "We Are Not Created Equal in Every Way." She writes of "disturbing issue[s]," lack of a "safety net" for young people on the star track to elite performance, and an absence of adults "watch[ing] out for [the children's] best interests." Ryan understands that no reader wants to see a child abused; and while she does not use the word *abuse* in her essay, she implies that parents who push young children too hard to succeed commit abuse. That implication is enough to engage the sympathies of the reader. As someone evaluating the essay, you should be alert to this appeal to your emotions and then judge whether or not the appeal is fair and convincing. Above all, you should not let an emotional appeal blind you to shortcomings of logic, ambiguously defined terms, or a misuse of facts.

***Ad Hominem* Argument.** In an *ad hominem* argument, the writer rejects opposing views by attacking the person who holds them. By calling opponents names, an author avoids the issue. Consider this excerpt from a political speech:

> I could more easily accept my opponent's plan to increase revenues by collecting on delinquent tax bills if he had paid more than a hundred dollars in state taxes in each of the past three years. But the fact is, he's a millionaire with a millionaire's tax shelters. This man hasn't paid a wooden nickel for the state services he and his family depend on. So I ask you: Is *he* the one to be talking about taxes to *us?*

It could well be that the opponent has paid virtually no state taxes for three years; but this fact has nothing to do with, and is used as a ploy to divert attention from, the merits of a specific proposal for increasing revenues. The proposal is lost in the attack against the man himself, an attack that violates principles of logic. Writers (and speakers) should make their points by citing evidence in support of their views and by challenging contrary evidence.

Does Ryan attack Fredrika Keefer's mother in this essay? You be the judge. Here are lines referring directly or indirectly to Krissy Keefer. Is Ryan criticizing the mother, directly or indirectly? Cite specific words and phrases to support your conclusion.

> Fredrika and her mother filed suit because, as her mother puts it, she "did not have the right body type to be accepted" by the San Francisco Ballet School. "My daughter is very sophisticated, so she understands why we're doing this," Krissy Keefer said. "And the other kids think she's a celebrity."

> There is no question Keefer raises a powerful point in her complaint.

> Keefer said she would drop her lawsuit if the school accepted her daughter. The San Francisco Ballet School offers the best training in the Bay Area, she said. Fredrika, however, has said she is quite happy dancing where she is. Still, the mother gets to decide what's best for her daughter's dancing career. The child is clearly too young to make such a decision. Yet, in the skewed logic of elite athletics and dancing, she is not too young to pay the price for it.

**Faulty Cause and Effect.** The fact that one event precedes another in time does not mean that the first event has caused the second. An example: Fish begin dying by the thousands in a lake near your hometown. An environmental group immediately cites chemical dumping by several manufacturing plants as the cause. But other causes are possible: A disease might have affected the fish; the growth of algae might have contributed to the deaths; or acid rain might be a factor. The origins of an event are usually complex and are not always traceable to a single cause. So you must carefully examine cause-and-effect reasoning when you find a writer

## TONE

Tone refers to the overall emotional effect produced by a writer's choice of language. Writers might use especially emphatic words to create a tone: A film reviewer might refer to a "magnificent performance," or a columnist might criticize "sleazeball politics."

These are extreme examples of tone; but tone can be more subtle, particularly if the writer makes a special effort *not* to inject emotion into the writing. As we've indicated above in the section on emotionally loaded terms, the fact that a writer's tone is highly emotional does not necessarily mean that the writer's argument is invalid. Conversely, a neutral tone does not ensure an argument's validity.

Note that many instructors discourage student writing that projects a highly emotional tone, considering it inappropriate for academic or preprofessional work. (One sure sign of emotion: the exclamation mark, which should be used sparingly.)

using it. In Latin, this fallacy is known as *post hoc, ergo propter hoc* ("after this, therefore because of this").

The debate over the San Francisco Ballet School's refusal to admit Fredrika Keefer involves a question of cause and effect. Fredrika Keefer's rejection by the ballet school was caused by the school's insistence that its students have an "ethereal, elongated body." If the school changes that standard, the outcome could change: Fredrika Keefer might be admitted.

Ryan also uses cause-and-effect logic in her essay to suggest that Fredrika Keefer's mother, and by extension all parent managers, can cause their children harm by pushing them too hard in their training. At the end of the essay, Ryan writes that Fredrika is too young "to decide what's best for her . . . dancing career" but that "she is not too young to pay the price for" the decisions her mother makes to promote that career. The "price" Fredrika pays will be "caused" by her mother's (poor) decisions.

**Either/Or Reasoning**. Either/or reasoning also results from an unwillingness to recognize complexity. If in analyzing a problem an author artificially restricts the range of possible solutions by offering only two courses of action, and then rejects the one that he opposes, he cannot logically argue that the remaining course of action, which he favors, is therefore the only one that makes sense. Usually, several other options (at least) are possible. For whatever reason, the author has chosen to overlook them. As an example, suppose you are reading a selection on genetic engineering in which the author builds an argument on the basis of the following:

> Research in gene splicing is at a crossroads: Either scientists will be carefully monitored by civil authorities and their efforts limited to acceptable applications, such as disease control; or, lacking regulatory guidelines, scientists will set their own ethical standards and begin programs in embryonic manipulation that, however well intended, exceed the proper limits of human knowledge.

Certainly, other possibilities for genetic engineering exist beyond the two mentioned here. But the author limits debate by establishing an either/or choice. Such a limitation is artificial and does not allow for complexity. As a critical reader, you need to be on the alert for either/or reasoning.

**Hasty Generalization.** Writers are guilty of hasty generalization when they draw their conclusions from too little evidence or from unrepresentative evidence. To argue that scientists should not proceed with the human genome project because a recent editorial urged that the project be abandoned is to make a hasty generalization. That lone editorial may be unrepresentative of the views of most individuals—both scientists and laypeople— who have studied and written about the matter. To argue that one should never obey authority because Stanley Milgram's Yale University experiments in the 1960s showed the dangers of obedience is to ignore the fact that Milgram's experiments were concerned primarily with obedience to *immoral* authority. Thus the experimental situation was unrepresentative of most routine demands for obedience—for example, to obey a parental rule or to comply with a summons for jury duty—and a conclusion about the malevolence of all authority would be a hasty generalization.

**False Analogy.** Comparing one person, event, or issue to another may be illuminating, but it can also be confusing or misleading. Differences between the two may be more significant than their similarities, and conclusions drawn from one may not necessarily apply to the other. A writer who argues that it is reasonable to quarantine people with AIDS because quarantine has been effective in preventing the spread of smallpox is assuming an analogy between AIDS and smallpox that is not valid (because of the differences in transmission between the two diseases).

Ryan compares the San Francisco Ballet School's setting an admissions standard to both a university's and a modeling school's setting standards. Are the analogies apt? Certainly one can draw a parallel between the standards used by the ballet school and those of a modeling school: Both emphasize a candidate's appearance, among other qualities. Are the admissions standards of a university based on appearance? In principle, no. At least that's not a criterion any college admissions office would post on its Web site. A critical reader might therefore want to object that one of Ryan's analogies is faulty.

Ryan attempts to advance her argument by making another comparison:

> [The rejection of a candidate because she does not have a body suited to classical ballet] doesn't mean that women with different body types cannot become professional dancers. They just have to find a different type of dance—jazz, tap, modern—just as athletes have to find sports that fit certain body types. A tall, blocky man, for example, could not be a jockey but he could play baseball.

The words "just as" signal an attempt to advance the argument by making an analogy. What do you think? Is the analogy sufficiently similar to Fredrika Keefer's situation to persuade you?

**Begging the Question.** To beg the question is to assume as proven fact the very thesis being argued. To assert, for example, that America is not in decline because it is as strong and prosperous as ever does not prove anything: It merely repeats the claim in different words. This fallacy is also known as *circular reasoning.*

When Ryan writes that "There is no safety net [for children placed into elite training programs], no arm of government that makes sure that the adults in their lives watch out for their best interests," she assumes that there should be such a safety net. But, as you will read in the sample critique, this is a point that must be argued, not assumed. Is such intervention wise? Under what circumstances would authorities intervene in a family? Would authorities have the legal standing to get involved if there were no clear evidence of physical abuse? Ryan is not necessarily wrong in desiring "safety nets" for young, elite athletes and dancers, but she assumes a point that she should be arguing.

*Non Sequitur.* *Non sequitur* is Latin for "it does not follow"; the term is used to describe a conclusion that does not logically follow from a premise. "Since minorities have made such great strides in the past few decades," a writer may argue, "we no longer need affirmative action programs." Aside from the fact that the premise itself is arguable (*have* minorities made such great strides?), it does not follow that because minorities *may* have made great strides, there is no further need for affirmative action programs.

**Oversimplification.** Be alert for writers who offer easy solutions to complicated problems. "America's economy will be strong again if we all 'buy American,'" a politician may argue. But the problems of America's economy are complex and cannot be solved by a slogan or a simple change in buying habits. Likewise, a writer who argues that we should ban genetic engineering assumes that simple solutions ("just say no") will be sufficient to deal with the complex moral dilemmas raised by this new technology.

## Writing to Entertain

Authors write not only to inform and persuade but also to entertain. One response to entertainment is a hearty laugh, but it is possible to entertain without encouraging laughter: A good book or play or poem may prompt you to reflect, grow wistful, become elated, get angry. Laughter is only one of many possible reactions. Like a response to an informative piece or an argument, your response to an essay, poem, story, play, novel, or film should be precisely stated and carefully developed. Ask yourself some of the following questions (you won't have space to explore all of them, but try to consider the most important): Did I care for the portrayal of a certain character? Did that character (or a group of characters united by occupation, age, ethnicity, etc.) seem overly sentimental, for example, or heroic? Did his adversaries seem too villainous or stupid? Were the situations believable? Was the action interesting or merely formulaic? Was the theme developed subtly or powerfully, or did the work come across as preachy or shrill? Did the action at the end of the work follow plausibly from what had come before? Was the language fresh and incisive or stale and predictable? Explain as specifically as possible what elements of the work seemed effective or ineffective and why. Offer an overall assessment, elaborating on your views.

## Question 2: To What Extent Do You Agree with the Author?

When formulating a critical response to a source, try to distinguish your evaluation of the author's purpose and success at achieving that purpose from your own agreement or disagreement with the author's views. The distinction allows you to respond to a piece of writing on its merits. As an unbiased, evenhanded critic, you evaluate an author's clarity of presentation, use of evidence, and adherence to principles of logic. To what extent has the author succeeded in achieving his or her purpose? Still withholding judgment, offer your assessment and give the author (in effect) a grade. Significantly, your assessment of the presentation may not coincide with your views of the author's conclusions: You may agree with an author entirely but feel that the presentation is superficial; you may find the author's logic and use of evidence to be rock solid but at the same time you may resist certain conclusions. A critical evaluation works well when it is conducted in two parts. After evaluating the author's purpose and design for achieving that purpose, respond to the author's main assertions. In doing so, you'll want to identify points of agreement and disagreement and also evaluate assumptions.

### Identify Points of Agreement and Disagreement

Be precise in identifying where you agree and disagree with an author. You should state as clearly as possible what *you* believe, and an effective way of doing this is to define your position in relation to that presented in the piece. Whether you agree enthusiastically, agree with reservations, or disagree, you can organize your reactions in two parts: (1) summarize the author's position; and (2) state your own position and elaborate on your reasons for holding it. The elaboration, in effect, becomes an argument itself, and this is true regardless of the position you take. An opinion is effective when you support it by supplying evidence from your reading (which should be properly cited), your observation, or your personal experience. Without such evidence, opinions cannot be authoritative. "I thought the article on inflation was lousy." Or: "It was terrific." Why? "I just thought so, that's all." This opinion is worthless because the criticism is imprecise: The critic has taken neither the time to read the article carefully nor the time to explore his or her own reactions carefully.

*Explore the Reasons for Agreement and Disagreement: Evaluate Assumptions*

One way of elaborating your reactions to a reading is to explore the underlying *reasons* for agreement and disagreement. Your reactions are based largely on assumptions that you hold and how these assumptions compare with the author's. An *assumption* is a fundamental statement about the world and its operations that you take to be true. A writer's assumptions may be explicitly stated; but just as often, assumptions are implicit and you can only infer them. Consider an example:

> *In vitro* fertilization and embryo transfer are brought about outside the bodies of the couple through actions of third parties whose competence and technical activity determine the success of the procedure. Such fertilization entrusts the life and identity of the embryo into the power of doctors and biologists and establishes the domination of technology over the origin and destiny of the human person. Such a relationship of domination is in itself contrary to the dignity and equality that must be common to parents and children.[*]

This paragraph is quoted from the February 1987 Vatican document on artificial procreation. Cardinal Joseph Ratzinger (now Pope Benedict XVI), the principal author of the document, makes an implicit assumption in this paragraph: No good can come of the domination of technology over conception: the use of technology to bring about conception is morally wrong. Yet thousands of childless couples, Roman Catholics included, have rejected this assumption in favor of its opposite: Conception technology can be an aid to the barren couple; far from creating a relationship of

---

[*] From the Vatican document *Instruction on Respect for Human Life in Its Origin and on the Dignity of Procreation*, given at Rome, from the *Congregation for the Doctrine of the Faith*, February 22, 1987, as presented in *Origins: N.C. Documentary Service* 16.40 (March 19, 1987): 707.

unequals, the technology brings children into the world who will be welcomed with joy and love.

Assumptions provide the foundation on which entire presentations are built. When you find an author's assumptions invalid—that is, not supported by factual evidence—or if you disagree with value-based assumptions underlying an author's position, you may well disagree with the conclusions that follow from these assumptions. The author of a book on developing nations may include a section outlining the time and resources and time that would be required to industrialize a particular country and so upgrade its general welfare. Her assumption—that industrialization in that particular country will ensure or even affect the general welfare—may or may not be valid. If you do not share the assumption, in your eyes the rationale for the entire book may be undermined.

How do you determine the validity of assumptions once you have identified them? In the absence of more scientific criteria, you may determine validity by how well the author's assumptions stack up against your own experience, observations, reading, and values. A caution, however: The overall value of an article or book may depend only to a small degree on the validity of the author's assumptions. For instance, a sociologist may do a fine job of gathering statistical data on the incidence of crime in urban areas along the eastern seaboard. The sociologist also might be a Marxist, and you may disagree with the subsequent analysis of the data. Yet you may still find the data extremely valuable for your own work.

Readers will want to examine two assumptions at the heart of Ryan's essay on Fredrika Keefer and the San Francisco Ballet School's refusal to admit her. First, Ryan assumes that setting a standard for admission based on a candidate's appearance is equivalent to setting a standard based on a candidate's "mental prowess," the admissions standard (presumably) used by universities. An appearance-based standard, Ryan writes, will "weed out those who are less likely to succeed" in professional ballet. The writer of the critique that follows agrees with Ryan's assumption. But you may not. You may assume, by contrast, that standards based on appearance are arbitrary while those based on intellectual ability rest on documented talent (SAT scores or high school transcripts, for instance). Ryan makes a second assumption: that there are appropriate and inappropriate ways to raise children. She does not state the ways explicitly, but that does not keep her from using them to judge Krissy Keefer harshly. You may disagree with her and find a reason to cheer Krissy Keefer's defense of her daughter's rights. That's your decision. What you must do as a critical reader is recognize assumptions whether they are stated or not. You should spell them out and then accept or reject them. Ultimately, your agreement or disagreement with an author will rest on your agreement or disagreement with the author's assumptions.

## CRITIQUE

In Chapter 1 we focused on summary—the condensed presentation of ideas from another source. Summary is key to much of academic writing because it relies so heavily on the works of others for the support of claims. It's not going too far to say that summarizing is the critical thinking skill from which a majority of academic writing builds. However, most academic thinking and writing do not stop at summary; usually we use summary to restate our understanding of things we see or read. Then we put that summary to use. In academic writing, one typical use of summary is as a prelude to critique.

A *critique* is a *formalized, critical reading of a passage*. It is also a personal response, but writing a critique is considerably more rigorous than saying that a movie is "great," or a book is "fascinating," or "I didn't like it." These are all responses, and, as such, they're a valid, even essential, part of your understanding of what you see and read. But such responses don't illuminate the subject —even for you—if you haven't explained how you arrived at your conclusions.

## GUIDELINES FOR WRITING CRITIQUES

- *Introduce.* Introduce both the passage under analysis and the author. State the author's main argument and the point(s) you intend to make about it.

  Provide background material to help your readers understand the relevance or appeal of the passage. This background material might include one or more of the following: an explanation of why the subject is of current interest; a reference to a possible controversy surrounding the subject of the passage or the passage itself; biographical information about the author; an account of the circumstances under which the passage was written; a reference to the intended audience of the passage.

- *Summarize.* Summarize the author's main points, making sure to state the author's purpose for writing.

- *Assess the presentation.* Evaluate the validity of the author's presentation, as distinct from your points of agreement or disagreement. Comment on the author's success in achieving his or her purpose by reviewing three or four specific points. You might base your review on one or more of the following criteria:

  Is the information accurate?

  Is the information significant?

  Has the author defined terms clearly?

  Has the author used and interpreted information fairly?

  Has the author argued logically?

- *Respond to the presentation.* Now it is your turn to respond to the author's views. With which views do you agree? With which do you disagree? Discuss your reasons for agreement and disagreement, when possible tying these reasons to assumptions—both the author's and your own. Where necessary, draw on outside sources to support your ideas.

- *Conclude*. State your conclusions about the overall validity of the piece—your assessment of the author's success at achieving his or her aims and your reactions to the author's views. Remind the reader of the weaknesses and strengths of the passage.

Your task in writing a critique is to turn your critical reading of a passage into a systematic evaluation in order to deepen your reader's (and your own) understanding of that passage. Among other things, you're interested in determining what an author says, how well the points are made, what assumptions underlie the argument, what issues are overlooked, and what implications can be drawn from such an analysis. Critiques, positive or negative, should include a fair and accurate summary of the passage; they may draw on and cite information and ideas from other sources (your reading or your personal experience and observations); and they should also include a statement of your own assumptions. It is important to remember that you bring to bear an entire set of assumptions about the world. Stated or not, these assumptions underlie every evaluative comment you make; you therefore have an obligation, both to the reader and to yourself, to clarify your standards by making your assumptions explicit. Not only do your readers stand to gain by your forthrightness, but so do you. In the process of writing a critical assessment, you are forced to examine your own knowledge, beliefs, and assumptions. Ultimately, the critique is a way of learning about yourself—yet another example of the ways in which writing is useful as a tool for critical thinking.

## How to Write Critiques

You may find it useful to organize a critique into five sections: introduction, summary, assessment of the presentation (on its own terms), your response to the presentation, and conclusion.

The box on pages 58–59 offers some guidelines for writing critiques. They do not constitute a rigid formula. Thousands of authors write critiques that do not follow the structure outlined here. Until you are more confident and practiced in writing critiques, however, we suggest you follow these guidelines. They are meant not to restrict you, but rather to provide a workable sequence for writing critiques.

## DEMONSTRATION: CRITIQUE

The critique that follows is based on Joan Ryan's "We Are Not Created Equal in Every Way," which appeared as an op-ed piece in *The San Francisco Chronicle* on December 12, 2000 (see pages 42–44), and which we have to some extent already begun to examine. In this formal critique, you will see that it is possible to agree with an author's main point, at least provisionally, yet disagree with other elements of the argument. Critiquing a different selection, you could just as easily accept the author's facts and figures but reject the conclusion he draws from them. As long as you carefully articulate the author's assumptions and your own, explaining in some detail your agreement and disagreement, the critique is yours to take in whatever direction you see fit.

Let's summarize the preceding sections by returning to the core questions that guide critical reading. You will see how, when applied to Joan Ryan's argument, they help to set up a critique.

### To What Extent Does the Author Succeed in His or Her Purpose?

To answer this question, you will need to know the author's purpose. Joan Ryan's "We Are Not Created Equal in Every Way" is an argument—actually, *two* related arguments. She wants readers to accept her view that (1) a school of performing arts has the right to set admissions standards according to criteria it believes will ensure the professional success of its graduates; and (2) parents may damage their children by pushing them too hard to meet the standards set by these schools.

By supporting a ballet school's right to set admission standards based on appearance, Ryan supports the star system that produces our elite athletes and performers. At the same time, she disapproves of parents who risk their children's safety and welfare by pushing them through this system. Ryan both defends the system and attacks it. Her ambivalence on the issue keeps the argument from succeeding fully.

## To What Extent Do You Agree with the Author?: Evaluate Assumptions

Ryan's views on the debate surrounding Fredrika Keefer's rejection by the San Francisco School of Ballet rest on the assumption that the school has the right to set its own admissions standards—even if we find those standards harsh. All private institutions, she claims, have that right. The writer of the critique that follows agrees with Ryan, although we have seen how it is possible to disagree.

Ryan's second argument concerns the wisdom of subjecting an 8-year-old to the rigors of professional training. Ryan disapproves. The writer of the critique, while sympathetic to Ryan's concerns, states that as a practical and even as a legal matter it would be nearly impossible to prevent parents such as Krissy Keefer from doing exactly as they please in the name of helping their children. In our culture, parents have the right (short of outright abuse) to raise children however they see fit.

Finally, the writer of the critique notes a certain ambivalence in Ryan's essay: her support of the ballet school's admission standards on the one hand and her distaste for parent managers like Krissy Keefer on the other. The writer does not find evidence of a weak argument in Ryan's mixed message but rather a sign of confusion in the broader culture: We love our young stars, but we condemn parents for pushing children to the breaking point in the name of stardom.

The selections you are likely to critique will be those, like Ryan's, that argue a specific position. Indeed, every argument you read is an invitation to agree or disagree. It remains only for you to speak up and justify your position.

## MODEL CRITIQUE

Ralston 1

Eric Ralston
Professor Reilly
Writing 2
11 January 2008

A Critique of "We Are Not Created Equal
in Every Way" by Joan Ryan

1    Most freshmen know how it feels to apply to a school and be rejected. Each year, college admissions offices mail thousands of thin letters that begin: "Thank you for your application. The competition this year was unusually strong. . . ." We know that we will not get into every college on our list or pass every test or win the starring role after every audition, but we believe that we deserve the chance to try. And we can tolerate rejection if we know that we compete on a level playing field. But when that field seems to arbitrarily favor some candidates over others, we take offense. At least that's when an ambitious mother took offense, bringing to court a suit that claimed her eight-year-old daughter, Fredrika Keefer, was denied admission to the prestigious San Francisco Ballet School because she had the wrong "body type" (A29).

2    In an opinion piece for the San Francisco Chronicle
(12 December 2000), Joan Ryan asks: "Does [a ballet
school] have the right to give preference to leaner body
types?" Her answer is a firm yes. Ryan argues that institutions have the right to set whatever standards they want
to ensure that those they admit meet the physical or intellectual requirements for professional success. But she
also believes that some parents push their children too
hard to meet those standards. Ryan offers a questionable
approach to protecting children from the possible abuses
of such parents. Overall, however, she raises timely issues
in discussing the star system that produces our world-
class athletes and performers. The sometimes conflicting
concerns she expresses reflect contradictions and ten-
sions in our larger culture.

3    The issue Ryan discusses is a particularly sensitive one
because the child's mother charged the ballet school with
discrimination. As a society we have made great strides
over the past few decades in combating some of the more
blatant forms of discrimination--racial, ethnic, and sexual.
But is it possible, is it desirable, to eliminate all efforts to
distinguish one person from another? When is a standard
that permits some (but not all) people entry to an institution discriminatory and when is it a necessary part of
doing business? Ryan believes that schools discriminate all
the time, and rightly so when candidates for admission fail
to meet the stated criteria for academic or professional success. That UC Berkeley does not accept every applicant is
discriminating, not discriminatory. Ryan recognizes the
difference.

4     She maintains, correctly, that the San Francisco Ballet
School, like any other private institution, has the right to set
standards by which it will accept or reject applicants.
Rejection is a part of life, she writes, expressing the view
that gives her essay its title: "We Are Not Created Equal in
Every Way." And because we are not created equal, not
everyone will be admitted to his or her number one school
or get a turn on stage. That's the inevitable consequence of
setting standards: Some people will meet them and gain
admission, others won't. Ryan quotes the spokesperson
who explained that the San Francisco Ballet School is "'not
a recreation department'" (A29). In other words, a professional ballet school, like a university, is within its rights to
reject applicants with body types unsuited to its view of
success in professional ballet. The standard may be cruel
and to some even arbitrary, but it is understandable. To put
the matter bluntly, candidates with unsuitable body types,
however talented or otherwise attractive, are less likely to
succeed in professional ballet than those with "classical"
proportions. Female dancers, for example, must regularly
be lifted and carried, as if effortlessly, by their male coun-
terparts--a feat that is difficult enough even with "leaner
body types." Ryan points out that candidates without the
ideal body type for ballet are not barred from professional
dance: "[t]hey just have to find a different type of dance . . .
just as athletes have to find sports that fit certain body
types" (A29).

5     The San Francisco Ballet School is not saying that
people of a certain skin color or religious belief are not
welcome. That would be discriminatory and wrong. But

the standard concerning body type cuts across <u>all</u> people,
rich or poor, black or white, Protestant or Jew, male or
female. Such a broad standard could be termed an equal
opportunity standard: If it can be used to distinguish
among all people equally, it is discriminating, not
discriminatory.

6    Ryan's parallel concern in this essay is the damage done to
children by parents who push them at an early age to meet the
high standards set by professional training programs. Children
placed onto such star tracks attend special schools (or receive
home schooling) in order to accommodate intense training
schedules that sometimes lead to physical or psychological
injuries. In healthy families, we might expect parents to
protect children from such dangers. But parents who manage
what they view as their children's "careers" may be too single-
minded to realize that their actions may place Johnny and
Susie at risk.

7    Ryan disapproves of a star track system that puts children into professional training at a young age. In pursuing
a career in dance, for instance, a young "child has thrown
all her eggs into this one little basket at an age when most
kids can barely decide what to wear to school in the morning" (A29). The law makes no provision for protecting
such elite performers in training, writes Ryan: "There is
no safety net for them, no arm of government that makes
sure that the adults in their lives watch out for their best
interests" (A29).

8    Like the rest of us, Ryan assumes there are appropriate
and less appropriate ways to raise children. While she
does not explicitly share her preferred approach, she uses

language effectively (both her own and her subjects') to
suggest what does not work: pushing an otherwise "quite
happy" eight-year-old who "relishes" dancing into professional ballet school. Ryan is subtle enough not to attack
Krissy Keefer directly, instead letting the mother undermine herself with a comment few could take seriously:
"My daughter is very sophisticated, so she understands
why we're [bringing a lawsuit]." No eight-year-old could
fully understand the motivations behind a lawsuit, and the
statement suggests a mother pursuing her own--not her
daughter's--agenda. Ryan suggests that Krissy Keefer has
succumbed to "the skewed logic of elite athletics and
dancing" that has damaged too many young people. When
Ryan points out that "no arm of government" looks out
for children like Frederika, she implies the need for a
Department of Youth Services to supervise parent managers. This is not a good idea.

9       There is no sure way to tell when a parent's managing of
a child's dance or athletic schedule is abusive or construc-
tive. Intense dedication is necessary for would-be elite athletes and performers to succeed, and such dedication often
begins in childhood. Since young children are not equipped
to organize their lives in pursuit of a single goal, parents
step in to help. That's what the parents of Tiger Woods did
on recognizing his talents:

>        [H]is father . . . [started] him very early. . . . [Tiger]
>        was on the Mike Douglas show hitting golf balls when
>        he was three years old. I mean, this is a prodigy type
>        thing. This is like Mozart writing his first symphony
>        when he was six, that sort of thing, and he did show

unique ability right from the beginning. And his life
has been channeled into being a pro. His father has
devoted his life to bringing him to this point. His
father hasn't worked full-time since 1988. That's what
it's been all about. (Feinstein)

10    Ryan would point out, correctly, that for every
Tiger Woods or Michelle Kwan there are many child-
athletes and performing artists who fall short of their
goals. They may later regret the single-minded focus that
robbed them of their childhood, but there is no way to
know before committing a child to years of dedicated
practice whether he or she will become the next Tiger or
an embittered also-ran. We simply do not have the wisdom
to intervene in a parent manager's training program for
her child. And Joan Ryan is not going to find an "arm of
government" to intervene in the child rearing of Fredrika
Keefer, however much she may "pay the price for" (A29)
her mother's enthusiasm.

11    The tension in Ryan's essay over high standards and the
intense preparation to meet them mirrors a tension in the
larger culture. On the one hand, Ryan argues persuasively
that elite institutions like the San Francisco Ballet
School have the right to set standards for admission. At such
institutions, high standards give us high levels of achieve-
ment--dancers, for instance, who "can float on air" (A29).
We cheer brilliant performers like Tiger Woods and Michelle
Kwan who started on their roads to success while still
children. The star system produces stars. On the other hand,
Ryan condemns parents who buy into the star system by
pushing their children into professional training programs

that demand a single-minded focus. We are horrified to learn that Macaulay Culkin of the <u>Home Alone</u> movies never really had a childhood (Peterson). Of course Culkin and others like him didn't have childhoods: They were too busy practicing their lines or their jumps and spins. If Ryan defends high standards in one breath and criticizes parents in the next for pushing children to achieve these standards, she is only reflecting a confusion in the larger culture: We love our stars, but we cannot have our stars without a star system that demands total (and often damaging) dedication from our youngest and most vulnerable citizens. That parents can be the agent of this damage is especially troubling.

12      Joan Ryan is right to focus on the parents of would-be stars, and she is right to remind us that young children pressured to perform at the highest levels can suffer physically and psychologically. Perhaps it was better for Fredrika Keefer the child (as opposed to Fredrika Keefer the future professional dancer) that she was not admitted to the San Francisco School of Ballet. For Keefer's sake and that of other child performers, we should pay attention to the dangers of the star system and support these children when we can. But without clear evidence of legally actionable neglect or abuse, we cannot interfere with parent managers, however much we may disagree with their decisions. We may be legitimately concerned, as is Ryan, that such a parent is driving her child to become not the next Tiger Woods but the next admission to a psychiatric ward. In a free society, for better or for worse, parents have the right to guide (or misguide) the lives of their children. All the rest of us can do is watch—and hope for the best.

Ralston 8

Works Cited

Feinstein, John. "Year of the Tiger." Interview with Jim
    Lehrer. Online News Hour. 14 Apr. 1997. 8 Jan.
    2008 <http://www.pbs.org/newshour/bb/sports/
    tiger_4-14.html>.

Peterson, Paul. Interview with Gary James. 12 Feb. 2000.
    8 Jan. 2008 <http://www.classicbands.com/
    PaulPetersonInterview.html>.

Ryan, Joan. "We Are Not Created Equal in Every
    Way." San Francisco Chronicle 12 Dec. 2000: A29.

## CRITICAL READING FOR CRITIQUE

- *Use the tips from Critical Reading for Summary on
  page 5.* Remember to examine the context; note the title
  and subtitle; identify the main point; identify the subpoints; break the reading into sections; distinguish
  between points, examples, and counterarguments;
  watch for transitions within and between paragraphs;
  and read actively.
- *Establish the writer's primary purpose in writing.* Is the
  piece meant primarily to inform, persuade, or entertain?
- *Evaluate informative writing. Use these criteria (among
  others):*

  Accuracy of information

  Significance of information

  Fair interpretation of information

  *(Continued on next page)*

- *Evaluate persuasive writing. Use these criteria (among others):*

  Clear definition of terms

  Fair use and interpretation of information

  Logical reasoning

- *Evaluate writing that entertains. Use these criteria (among others):*

  Interesting characters

  Believable action, plot, and situations

  Communication of theme

  Use of language

- *Decide whether you agree or disagree with the writer's ideas, position, or message.* Once you have determined the extent to which an author has achieved his or her purpose, clarify your position in relation to the writer's.

## The Strategy of the Critique

- Paragraph 1 of the model critique introduces the issue to be reviewed. It provides brief background information and sets a general context that explains why the topic of fair (and unfair) competition is important.

- Paragraph 2 introduces the author and the essay and summarizes the author's main claims. The paragraph ends (see the final three sentences) with the writer's overall assessment of the essay.

- Paragraph 3 sets a specific context for evaluating Ryan's first claim concerning admissions standards. The writer summarizes Ryan's position by making a distinction between the terms *discriminating* and *discriminatory*.

- Paragraph 4 evaluates Ryan's first claim, that the ballet school has the right to set admission standards. The writer supports Ryan's position.

- Paragraph 5 continues the evaluation of Ryan's first claim. Again, the writer of the critique supports Ryan, returning to the distinction between *discriminating* and *discriminatory*.

- Paragraphs 6–7 summarize Ryan's second claim, that parents can damage their children by pushing them too hard through professional training programs at too early an age.

- Paragraphs 8–10 evaluate Ryan's second claim. In paragraph 8 the writer states that Ryan makes a mistake in implying that a government agency should safeguard the interests of children like Fredrika Keefer. Paragraphs 9–10 present the logic for disagreeing with Ryan on this point.

- Paragraph 11 evaluates the essay as a whole. Ryan defends the right of schools in the star system to set high standards but objects when parents push young children into this system. This "tension" in the essay reflects a confusion in the larger culture.

- Paragraph 12 concludes the critique. The writer offers qualified support of Ryan's position, agreeing that children caught in the star system can suffer. The writer also states that there is not much we can do about the problem except watch and hope for the best.

# 3

# Synthesis

## WHAT IS A SYNTHESIS?

A *synthesis* is a written discussion that draws on two or more sources. It follows that your ability to write syntheses depends on your ability to infer relationships among sources—essays, articles, fiction, and also nonwritten sources such as lectures, interviews, visual media, and observations. This process is nothing new for you because you infer relationships all the time—say, between something you've read in the newspaper and something you've seen for yourself, or between the teaching styles of your favorite and least favorite instructors. In fact, if you've written research papers, you've already written syntheses. In a *synthesis,* you make explicit the relationships that you have inferred among separate sources.

The skills you've already learned and practiced in the previous two chapters will be vital in writing syntheses. Before you're in a position to draw relationships between two or more sources, you must understand what those sources say; you must be able to *summarize* those sources. Readers will frequently benefit from at least partial summaries of sources in your synthesis essays. At the same time, you must go beyond summary to make judgments— judgments based on your *critical reading* of your sources: what conclusions you've drawn about the quality and validity of these sources, whether you agree or disagree with the points made in your sources, and why you agree or disagree.

In a synthesis, you go beyond the critique of individual sources to determine the relationships among them. Is the information in source B, for example, an extended illustration of the generalizations in source A? Would it be useful to compare and contrast source C with source B? Having read and considered sources A, B, and C, can you infer something else— in other words, D (not a source, but your own idea)?

Because a synthesis is based on two or more sources, you will need to be selective when choosing information from each. It would be neither possible nor desirable, for instance, to discuss in a ten-page paper on the American Civil War every point that the authors of two books make about their subject. What you as a writer must do is select from each source the ideas and information that best allow you to achieve your purpose.

## PURPOSE

Your purpose in reading source materials and then drawing on them to write your own material is often reflected in the wording of an assignment. For instance, consider the following assignments on the Civil War:

*American History:* Evaluate the author's treatment of the origins of the Civil War.

*Economics:* Argue the following proposition, in light of your readings: "The Civil War was fought not for reasons of moral principle but for reasons of economic necessity."

*Government:* Prepare a report on the effects of the Civil War on Southern politics at the state level between 1870 and 1917.

*Mass Communications:* Discuss how the use of photography during the Civil War may have affected the perceptions of the war by Northerners living in industrial cities.

---

## WHERE DO WE FIND WRITTEN SYNTHESES?

*Here are just a few of the types of writing that involve synthesis*

### Academic Writing

- **Analysis papers** synthesize and apply several related theoretical approaches.
- **Research papers** synthesize multiple sources.
- **Argument papers** synthesize different points into a coherent claim or position.
- **Essay exams** demonstrate understanding of course material through comparing and contrasting theories, viewpoints, or approaches in a particular field.

### Workplace Writing

- **Newspaper and magazine articles** synthesize primary and secondary sources.
- **Position papers and policy briefs** compare and contrast solutions for solving problems.
- **Business plans** synthesize ideas and proposals into one coherent plan.
- **Memos and letters** synthesize multiple ideas, events, and proposals into concise form.
- **Web sites** synthesize information from various sources to present in Web pages and related links.

---

*Literature:* Select two Southern writers of the twentieth-century whose work you believe was influenced by the divisive effects of the Civil War. Discuss the ways this influence is apparent in a novel or a group of short stories written by each author. The works should not be *about* the Civil War.

*Applied Technology:* Compare and contrast the technology of warfare available in the 1860s with the technology available a century earlier.

Each of these assignments creates a particular purpose for writing. Having located sources relevant to your topic, you would select for possible use in a paper only the parts of those sources that helped you in fulfilling this purpose. And how you used those parts—how you related them to other material from other sources—would also depend on your purpose. For instance, if you were working on the government assignment, you might draw on the same source as a student working on the literature assignment by referring to Robert Penn Warren's novel *All the King's Men*, about Louisiana politics in the early part of the twentieth century. But because the purposes of the two assignments are different, you and the other student would make different uses of this source. The parts or aspects of the novel that you find worthy of detailed analysis might be mentioned only in passing—or not at all—by the other student.

## USING YOUR SOURCES

Your purpose determines not only what parts of your sources you will use but also how you will relate them to one another. Since the very essence of synthesis is the combining of information and ideas, you must have some basis on which to combine them. *Some relationships among the material in your sources must make them worth synthesizing.* It follows that the better able you are to discover such relationships, the better able you will be to use your sources in writing syntheses. Notice that the mass communications assignment requires you to draw a *cause-and-effect* relationship between photographs of the war and

Northerners' perceptions of the war. The applied technology assignment requires you to *compare and contrast* state-of-the-art weapons technology in the eighteenth and nineteenth centuries. The economics assignment requires you to *argue* a proposition. In each case, *your purpose will determine how you relate your source materials to one another.*

Consider some other examples. You may be asked on an exam question or in the instructions for a paper to *describe* two or three approaches to prison reform during the past decade. You may be asked to *compare and contrast* one country's approach to imprisonment with another's. You may be asked to *develop an argument* of your own on this subject, based on your reading. Sometimes (when you are not given a specific assignment) you determine your own purpose: You are interested in exploring a particular subject; you are interested in making a case for one approach or another. In any event, your purpose shapes your essay. Your purpose determines which sources you research, which ones you use, which parts of them you use, at which points in your paper you use them, and in what manner you relate them to one another.

## TYPES OF SYNTHESES: ARGUMENT AND EXPLANATORY

In this chapter we categorize syntheses into two main types: *argument* and *explanatory*. The easiest way to recognize the difference between the two types may be to consider the difference between a news article and an editorial on the same subject. For the most part, we'd say that the main purpose of the news article is to convey *information,* and the main purpose of the editorial is to convey *opinion* or *interpretation.* Of course, this distinction is much too simplified: News articles often convey opinion or bias, sometimes subtly, sometimes openly; and editorials often convey unbiased information along with opinion. But as a practical matter we can generally agree on the distinction between a news article that primarily conveys information and an editorial that primarily conveys opinion. You should be able to observe this distinction in the selections shown here as Explanation and Argument.

### *Explanation: News article from the* New York Times

## Private Gets 3 Years for Iraq Prison Abuse

### By David S. Cloud

*September 28, 2005*

1   Pfc. Lynndie R. England, a 22-year-old clerk in the Army who was photographed with naked Iraqi detainees at Abu Ghraib prison, was sentenced on Tuesday to three years in prison and a dishonorable discharge for her role in the scandal.

2     After the sentence was announced, Private England hung her head and cried briefly before hugging her mother, one of the few signs of emotion she showed in the six-day trial.

3     She had been found guilty on Monday of one count of conspiracy to maltreat prisoners, four counts of maltreatment and one count of committing an indecent act.

4     She made no comment on Tuesday as she was led out of the courthouse in handcuffs and leg shackles.

5     Earlier in the day, though, she took the stand and apologized for abusing the prisoners, saying her conduct was influenced by Specialist Charles A. Graner Jr., her boyfriend at the time.

6     She said she was "embarrassed" when photographs showing her posing next to naked detainees became public in 2004.

7     "I was used by Private Graner," she said. "I didn't realize it at the time."

8     Specialist Graner was reduced in rank after he was convicted in January as ringleader of the abuse.

9     Often groping for words and staring downward, Private England directed her apology to the detainees and to any American troops and their families who might have been injured or killed as a result of the insurgency in Iraq gaining strength.

10    Prosecutors argued on Tuesday that the anti-American feeling generated in Arab and Muslim countries by the Abu Ghraib scandal justified sentencing Private England to four to six years in prison and dishonorably discharging her from the Army. The charges the jury found her guilty of on Monday carried a maximum penalty of nine years. . . .

---

### Argument: *Editorial from the* Boston Globe

**Military Abuse**

*September 28, 2005*

1  The court-martial conviction Monday of reservist Lynndie England for her role in the abuse of Iraqi prisoners at Abu Ghraib should fool no one that the Pentagon is taking seriously the mistreatment of Iraqis, especially after the release last Friday of a report on torture by members of the 82d Airborne Division stationed near Fallujah. . . .

2    If the [new] allegations are found credible, they further demolish the contention by officials that the abuse first reported at Abu Ghraib in 2004 was an isolated case of a few bad apples. Pentagon brass also tried to explain away the activities of England's unit as the actions of relatively untrained reservists. It is less easy to dismiss as a fluke such abuse when it occurs at the hands of the 82d Airborne, a thoroughly trained and highly decorated division.

3    The new charges, along with other accusations of abuse that have emerged since Abu Ghraib, including 28 suspicious detainee deaths, provide strong evidence that both reservist and active duty troops throughout Iraq were confused about their responsibility to treat detainees as prisoners of war under the terms of the Geneva Conventions. . . . Congress should have long since created a special commission, as proposed in a bill by Senator Carl Levin of Michigan, to investigate the issue of prisoner abuse. . . .

4    A truly independent inquiry, along the lines of the one done by the 9/11 commission, could trace accountability for prisoner abuse through statements and policies by ranking civilian and military officials in the Bush administration. Accountability for the shame of prisoner torture and abuse should not stop with Lynndie England and her cohort.

---

We'll say, for the sake of convenience, that the news article provides an *explanation* of England's sentence and that the editorial provides an *argument* for investigating responsibility *beyond* England.

As a further example of the distinction between explanation and argument, read the following paragraph:

> Researchers now use recombinant DNA technology to analyze genetic changes. With this technology, they cut and splice DNA from different species, then insert the modified molecules into bacteria or other types of cells that engage in rapid replication and cell division. The cells copy the foreign DNA right along with their own. In short order, huge populations produce useful quantities of recombinant DNA molecules. The new technology also is the basis of genetic engineering, by which genes are isolated, modified, and inserted back into the same organism or into a different one.*

Now read this paragraph:

> Many in the life sciences field would have us believe that the new gene splicing technologies are irrepressible and irreversible and that any attempt to oppose their introduction is both futile and retrogressive. They never stop to even consider the possibility that the new genetic science might be used in a wholly different manner than is currently being proposed. The fact is, the corporate agenda is only one of two potential paths into the Biotech Century. It is possible that the growing number of anti-eugenic

---

* Cecie Starr and Ralph Taggart, "Recombinant DNA and Genetic Engineering," *Biology: The Unity and Diversity of Life* (New York: Wadsworth, 1998).

activists around the world might be able to ignite a global debate around alternative uses of the new science—approaches that are less invasive, more sustainable and humane and that conserve and protect the genetic rights of future generations.[†]

Both of these passages deal with the topic of biotechnology, but the two take quite different approaches. The first passage comes from a biology textbook, while the second appears in a magazine article. As we might expect from a textbook on the broad subject of biology, the first passage is explanatory and informative; it defines and explains some of the key concepts of biotechnology without taking a position or providing commentary about the implications of the technology. Magazine articles often present information in the same ways; however, many magazine articles take specific positions, as we see in the second passage. This passage is argumentative or persuasive: its primary purpose is to convey a point of view regarding the topic of biotechnology.

While each of these excerpts presents a clear instance of writing that is either explanatory or argumentative, it is important to note that both sources for these excerpts—the textbook chapter and the magazine article—contain elements of both explanation and argument. The textbook writers, while they refrain from taking a particular position, do note the controversies surrounding biotechnology and genetic engineering. They might even subtly reveal a certain bias in favor of one side of the issue, through their word choice and tone, and perhaps through devoting more space and attention to one point of view. Explanatory and argumentative writing are not mutually exclusive. The overlap of explanation and argument is also found in the magazine article: In order to make his case against genetic engineering, the writer has to explain certain elements of the issue. Yet even while these categories overlap to a certain extent, the second passage

---

[†] Jeremy Rifkin, "The Ultimate Therapy: Commercial Eugenics on the Eve of the Biotech Century," *Tikkun* May-June 1998: 35.

clearly has argument as its primary purpose, and the first passage is primarily explanatory.

In Chapter 2 we noted that the primary purpose in a piece of writing may be informative, persuasive, or entertaining (or some combination of the three). Some scholars of writing argue that all writing is essentially persuasive, and even without entering into that complex argument, we've just seen how the varying purposes in writing do overlap. In order to persuade others of a particular position, we typically must inform them about it; conversely, a primarily informative piece of writing must also work to persuade the reader that its claims are truthful. Both informative and persuasive writing often include entertaining elements, and writing intended primarily to entertain also typically contains information and persuasion. For practical purposes, however, it is possible—and useful—to identify the *primary* purpose in a piece of writing as informative/explanatory, persuasive/argumentative, or entertaining. Entertainment as a primary purpose is the one least often practiced in purely academic writing—perhaps to your disappointment!—but information and persuasion are ubiquitous. So, while recognizing the overlap that will occur between these categories, we distinguish in this chapter between two types of synthesis writing: explanatory (or informative) and argument (or persuasive). Just as distinguishing the primary purpose in a piece of writing helps you to critically read and evaluate it, distinguishing the primary purpose in your own writing will help you to make the appropriate choices regarding your approach.

We'll first present guidelines for writing syntheses in general and then focus on the argument synthesis. Toward the end of the chapter, we'll discuss the explanatory synthesis.

## HOW TO WRITE SYNTHESES

Although writing syntheses can't be reduced to a lockstep method, it should help you to follow the guidelines listed in the box below.

## GUIDELINES FOR WRITING SYNTHESES

- *Consider your purpose in writing.* What are you trying to accomplish in your paper? How will this purpose shape the way you approach your sources?
- *Select and carefully read your sources,* according to your purpose. Then reread the passages, mentally summarizing each. Identify those aspects or parts of your sources that will help you fulfill your purpose. When rereading, *label* or *underline* the sources for main ideas, key terms, and any details you want to use in the synthesis.
- *Take notes on your reading.* In addition to labeling or underlining key points in the readings, you might write brief one- or two-sentence summaries of each source. This will help you in formulating your thesis statement and in choosing and organizing your sources later.
- *Formulate a thesis.* Your thesis is the main idea that you want to present in your synthesis. It should be expressed as a complete sentence. You might do some predrafting about the ideas discussed in the readings in order to help you work out a thesis. If you've written one-sentence summaries of the readings, looking them over will help you to brainstorm connections between readings and to devise a thesis.

    When you write your synthesis drafts, you will need to consider where your thesis fits in your paper. Sometimes the thesis is the first sentence, but more often it is *the final sentence of the first paragraph.* If you are writing an *inductively arranged* synthesis (see p. 100), the thesis sentence may not appear until the final paragraphs.
- *Decide how you will use your source material.* How will the information and the ideas in the passages help you fulfill your purpose?

- *Develop an organizational plan,* according to your thesis. How will you arrange your material? It is not necessary to prepare a formal outline. But you should have some plan that will indicate the order in which you will present your material and that will indicate the relationships among your sources.
- *Draft the topic sentences for the main sections.* This is an optional step, but you may find it a helpful transition from organizational plan to first draft.
- *Write the first draft* of your synthesis, following your organizational plan. Be flexible with your plan, however. Frequently, you will use an outline to get started. As you write, you may discover new ideas and make room for them by adjusting the outline. When this happens, reread your work frequently, making sure that your thesis still accounts for what follows and that what follows still logically supports your thesis.
- *Document your sources.* You must do this by crediting sources within the body of the synthesis—citing the author's last name and the page number from which the point was taken—and then providing full citation information in a list of "Works Cited" at the end. Don't open yourself to charges of plagiarism! (See pp.34–36.)
- *Revise your synthesis,* inserting transitional words and phrases where necessary. Make sure that the synthesis reads smoothly, logically, and clearly from beginning to end. Check for grammatical correctness, punctuation, and spelling.

**Note:** *The writing of syntheses is a recursive process, and you should accept a certain amount of backtracking and reformulating as inevitable. For instance, in developing an organizational plan (Step 6 of the procedure), you may discover a gap in your presentation that will send you scrambling for another source—back to Step 2. You may find that formulating a thesis and making*

*(Continued on next page)*

> *inferences among sources occur simultaneously; indeed, infer-*
> *ences are often made before a thesis is formulated. Our*
> *recommendations for writing syntheses will give you a structure*
> *that will get you started. But be flexible in your approach;*
> *expect discontinuity and, if possible, be assured that through*
> *backtracking and reformulating you will produce a coherent,*
> *well-crafted paper.*

# THE ARGUMENT SYNTHESIS

It's likely that most of the papers you'll be writing in the next few years will be focused on developing support for particular positions or claims, so we'll consider the argument synthesis first and in more detail. An argument synthesis is *persuasive* in purpose: *Welfare reform has largely succeeded* (or *failed*). Writers working with the same source material might conceive of and support different, opposing theses. So the thesis for an argument synthesis is a claim about which reasonable people could disagree. It is a claim with which—given the right arguments—your audience might be persuaded to agree. The strategy of your argument synthesis is therefore to find and use convincing *support* for your *claim*.

## The Elements of Argument: Claim, Support, and Assumption

One way of looking at an argument is to see it as an interplay of three essential elements: claim, support, and assumption. A *claim* is a proposition or conclusion that you are trying to prove. You prove this claim by using *support* in the form of fact or expert opinion. Linking your supporting evidence to your claim is your *assumption* about the subject. This assumption, also called a *warrant*, is—as we've discussed in Chapter 2—an underlying belief or principle about some aspect of the world and how it operates. By nature, assumptions (which are often unstated) tend to be more general than either claims or supporting evidence.

Here are the essential elements of an argument advocating parental restriction of television viewing for their high school children:

*Claim*
High school students should be restricted to no more than two hours of TV viewing per day.

*Support*
An important new study and the testimony of educational specialists reveal that students who watch more than two hours of TV a night have, on average, lower grades than those who watch less TV.

*Assumption*
Excessive TV viewing adversely affects academic performance.

For another example, here's an argumentative claim on the topic of what some call computer-mediated communication (CMC):

CMC threatens to undermine human intimacy, connection, and ultimately community.

Here are the elements of this argument:

*Support*
- While the Internet presents us with increased opportunities to meet people, these meetings are limited by geographical distance.
- People are spending increasing amounts of time in cyberspace: In 1998, the average Internet user spent over four hours per week online, a figure that has nearly doubled recently.

- College health officials report that excessive Internet usage threatens many college students' academic and psychological well-being.
- New kinds of relationships fostered on the Internet often pose challenges to pre-existing relationships.

*Assumptions*

- The communication skills used and the connections formed during Internet contact fundamentally differ from those used and formed during face-to-face contact.
- "Real" connection and a sense of community are sustained by face-to-face contact, not by Internet interactions.

For the most part, arguments should be constructed logically so that assumptions link evidence (supporting facts and expert opinions) to claims. As we'll see, however, logic is only one component of effective arguments.

## DEMONSTRATION: DEVELOPING AN ARGUMENT SYNTHESIS—BALANCING PRIVACY AND SAFETY IN THE WAKE OF VIRGINIA TECH

To demonstrate how to plan and draft an argument synthesis, let's consider another subject. If you were taking a course on Law and Society or Political Science or (from the Philosophy Department) Theories of Justice, you might find yourself considering the competing claims of privacy and public safety. The tension between these two highly prized values burst anew into public consciousness in 2007 after a mentally disturbed student at the Virginia Polytechnic Institute shot to death 32 fellow students and faculty members and injured 17 more. Unfortunately, this incident was only the latest in a long history of mass killings at American

schools.* It was later revealed that the shooter had a documented history of mental instability, but because of privacy
rules this information was not made available to university
officials. Many people demanded to know why this information was not shared with campus police or other officials
so that Virginia Tech could take measures to protect members of the university community. Didn't the safety of those
who were injured and killed outweigh the privacy of the
shooter? At what point, if any, *does* the right to privacy
outweigh the right to safety? What *should* the university have
done before the killing started? Should federal and state laws
on privacy be changed or even abandoned in the wake of
this and other similar incidents?

Suppose, in preparing to write a paper on balancing privacy and safety, you located (among others) the following
sources:

- *Mass Shootings at Virginia Tech, April 16, 2007: Report of the
  Review Panel Presented to Governor Kaine, Commonwealth of
  Virginia*, August 2007 (a report)
- "Virginia Tech Massacre Has Altered Campus Mental
  Health Systems"( a news article)
- The Family Educational Rights and Privacy Act (FERPA),
  sec.1232g (a federal statute)

Read these sources (which follow) carefully, noting as you
do the kinds of information and ideas you could draw upon
to develop an *argument synthesis*. Note: to save space and for
the purpose of demonstration, two of the three passages are
excerpts only. In preparing your paper, you would draw upon
entire articles, reports, and book chapters from which they
were taken. And you would draw upon more sources
than these in your search for supporting materials (as the

---

* In 1966 a student at the University of Texas at Austin, shooting from the campus
clock tower, killed 14 people and wounded 31. In 2006, a man shot and killed 5 girls
at an Amish school in Lancaster, Pennsylvania.

writer of the example synthesis has done; see pp. 114–115). But these three sources provide a good introduction to the subject. Our discussion of how these passages can form the basis of an argument synthesis resumes on p. 98.

### Mass Shootings at Virginia Tech, April 16, 2007

#### Report of the Review Panel
#### Presented to Governor Kaine, Commonwealth of Virginia, August 2007

*The following passage leads off the official report of the Virginia Tech shootings by the panel appointed by Virginia Governor Tim Kaine to investigate the incident. The mission of the panel was "to provide an independent, thorough, and objective incident review of this tragic event, including a review of educational laws, policies and institutions, the public safety and health care procedures and responses, and the mental health delivery system." Panel members included the chair, Colonel Gerald Massenghill, former Virginia State Police Superintendent; Tom Ridge, former Director of Homeland Security and former governor of Pennsylvania; Gordon Davies; Dr. Roger L. Depue; Dr. Aradhana A. "Bela" Sood; Judge Diane Strickland; and Carol L. Ellis. The panel Web site may be found at <http://www.vtreviewpanel.org/panel_info/>.*

### Summary Of Key Findings

1   On April 16, 2007, Seung Hui Cho, an angry and disturbed student, shot to death 32 students and faculty of Virginia Tech, wounded 17 more, and then killed himself.

2   The incident horrified not only Virginians, but people across the United States and throughout the world.

3   Tim Kaine, Governor of the Commonwealth of Virginia, immediately appointed a panel to review the events leading up to this tragedy; the handling of the incidents by public safety officials, emergency services providers, and the university; and the services subsequently provided to families, survivors, caregivers, and the community.

4    The Virginia Tech Review Panel reviewed several separate but related issues in assessing events leading to the mass shootings and their aftermath:

- The life and mental health history of Seung Hui Cho, from early childhood until the weeks before April 16.
- Federal and state laws concerning the privacy of health and education records.
- Cho's purchase of guns and related gun control issues.
- The double homicide at West Ambler Johnston (WAJ) residence hall and the mass shootings at Norris Hall, including the responses of Virginia Tech leadership and the actions of law enforcement officers and emergency responders.
- Emergency medical care immediately following the shootings, both onsite at Virginia Tech and in cooperating hospitals.
- The work of the Office of the Chief Medical Examiner of Virginia.
- The services provided for surviving victims of the shootings and others injured, the families and loved ones of those killed and injured, members of the university community, and caregivers.

5    The panel conducted over 200 interviews and reviewed thousands of pages of records, and reports the following major findings:

1. Cho exhibited signs of mental health problems during his childhood. His middle and high schools responded well to these signs and, with his parents' involvement, provided services to address his issues. He also received private psychiatric treatment and counseling for selective mutism and depression.

   In 1999, after the Columbine shootings, Cho's middle school teachers observed suicidal and homicidal ideations in his writings and recommended psychiatric counseling, which he received. It was at this point that he received medication for a short time. Although Cho's parents were aware that he was troubled at this time, they state they did not specifically know that he thought about homicide shortly after the 1999 Columbine school shootings.

2. During Cho's junior year at Virginia Tech, numerous incidents occurred that were clear warnings of mental instability. Although various individuals and departments within the university knew about each of these incidents, the university did not intervene effectively. No one knew all the information and no one connected all the dots.

3. University officials in the office of Judicial Affairs, Cook Counseling Center, campus police, the Dean of Students, and others explained their failures to communicate with one another or with Cho's parents by noting their belief that such communications are prohibited by the federal laws governing the privacy of health and education records. In reality, federal laws and their state counterparts afford ample leeway to share information in potentially dangerous situations.

4. The Cook Counseling Center and the university's Care Team failed to provide needed support and services to Cho during a period in late 2005 and early 2006. The system failed for lack of resources, incorrect interpretation of privacy laws, and passivity. Records of Cho's minimal treatment at Virginia Tech's Cook Counseling Center are missing.

5. Virginia's mental health laws are flawed and services for mental health users are inadequate. Lack of sufficient resources results in gaps in the mental health system including short term crisis stabilization and comprehensive outpatient services. The involuntary commitment process is challenged by unrealistic time constraints, lack of critical psychiatric data and collateral information, and barriers (perceived or real) to open communications among key professionals.

6. There is widespread confusion about what federal and state privacy laws allow. Also, the federal laws governing records of health care provided in educational settings are not entirely compatible with those governing other health records.

7. Cho purchased two guns in violation of federal law. The fact that in 2005 Cho had been judged to be a danger to himself and ordered to outpatient treatment made him ineligible to purchase a gun under federal law.

8. Virginia is one of only 22 states that report any information about mental health to a federal database used to conduct background checks on would-be gun purchasers. But Virginia law did not clearly require that persons such as Cho—who had been ordered into out-patient treatment but not committed to an institution—be reported to the database. Governor Kaine's executive order to report all persons involuntarily committed for outpatient treatment has temporarily addressed this ambiguity in state law. But a change is needed in the Code of Virginia as well.

9. Some Virginia colleges and universities are uncertain about what they are permitted to do regarding the possession of firearms on campus.

10. On April 16, 2007, the Virginia Tech and Blacksburg police departments responded quickly to the report of shootings at West Ambler Johnston residence hall, as did the Virginia Tech and Blacksburg rescue squads. Their responses were well coordinated.

11. The Virginia Tech police may have erred in prematurely concluding that their initial lead in the double homicide was a good one, or at least in conveying that impression to university officials while continuing their investigation. They did not take sufficient action to deal with what might happen if the initial lead proved erroneous. The police reported to the university emergency Policy Group that the "person of interest" probably was no longer on campus.

12. The VTPD erred in not requesting that the Policy Group issue a campus-wide notification that two persons had been killed and that all students and staff should be cautious and alert.

13. Senior university administrators, acting as the emergency Policy Group, failed to issue an all-campus notification about the WAJ killings until almost 2 hours had elapsed. University practice may have conflicted with written policies.

14. The presence of large numbers of police at WAJ led to a rapid response to the first 9-1-1 call that shooting had begun at Norris Hall.

15. Cho's motives for the WAJ or Norris Hall shootings are unknown to the police or the panel. Cho's writings and video-taped pronouncements do not explain why he struck when and where he did.

16. The police response at Norris Hall was prompt and effective, as was triage and evacuation of the wounded. Evacuation of others in the building could have been implemented with more care.

17. Emergency medical care immediately following the shootings was provided very effectively and timely both onsite and at the hospitals, although providers from different agencies had some difficulty communicating with one another. Communication of accurate information to hospitals standing by to receive the wounded and injured was somewhat deficient early on. An emergency operations center at Virginia Tech could have improved communications.

18. The Office of the Chief Medical Examiner properly discharged the technical aspects of its responsibility (primarily autopsies and identification of the deceased). Communication with families was poorly handled.

19. State systems for rapidly deploying trained professional staff to help families get information, crisis intervention, and referrals to a wide range of resources did not work.

20. The university established a family assistance center at The Inn at Virginia Tech, but it fell short in helping families and others for two reasons: lack of leadership and lack of coordination among service providers. University volunteers stepped in but were not trained or able to answer many questions and guide families to the resources they needed.

21. In order to advance public safety and meet public needs, Virginia's colleges and universities need to work together as a coordinated system of state-supported institutions.

6    As reflected in the body of the report, the panel has made more than 70 recommendations directed to colleges, universities, mental health providers, law enforcement officials, emergency service providers, lawmakers, and other public officials in Virginia and elsewhere.

## Virginia Tech Massacre Has Altered Campus Mental Health Systems

*This article, prepared by the Associated Press, is representative of numerous reports of how college administrators across the nation responded to the Virginia Tech killings. Many schools reviewed their existing policies on student privacy and communication and instituted new procedures. The article appeared in the* Los Angeles Times *on April 14, 2008.*

1    The rampage carried out nearly a year ago by a Virginia Tech student who slipped through the mental health system has changed how American colleges reach out to troubled students.

2    Administrators are pushing students harder to get help, looking more aggressively for signs of trouble and urging faculty to speak up when they have concerns. Counselors say the changes are sending even more students their way, which is both welcome and a challenge, given that many still lack the resources to handle their growing workloads.

3    Behind those changes, colleges have edged away in the last year from decades-old practices that made student privacy paramount. Now, they are more likely to err on the side of sharing information—with the police, for instance, and parents—if there is any possible threat to community safety. But even some who say the changes are appropriate worry it could discourage students from seeking treatment.

4    Concerns also linger that the response to shooters like Seung-hui Cho at Virginia Tech and Steven Kazmierczak, who killed five others at Northern Illinois University, has focused excessively on boosting the capacity of campus police to respond to rare events. Such reforms may be worthwhile, but they don't address how to prevent such a tragedy in the first place.

5    It was last April 16, just after 7 a.m., that Cho killed two students in a Virginia Tech dormitory, the start of a shooting spree

that continued in a classroom building and eventually claimed 33 lives, including his own.

6    Cho's behavior and writing had alarmed professors and administrators, as well as the campus police, and he had been put through a commitment hearing where he was found to be potentially dangerous. But when an off-campus psychiatrist sent him back to the school for outpatient treatment, there was no follow-up to ensure that he got it.

7    People who work every day in the campus mental health field—counselors, lawyers, advocates and students at colleges around the country—say they have seen three major types of change since the Cho shootings:

8    Faculty are speaking up more about students who worry them. That's accelerating a trend of more demand for mental health services that was already under way before the Virginia Tech shootings.

9    Professors "have a really heightened level of fear and concern from the behavior that goes on around them," said Ben Locke, assistant director of the counseling center at Penn State University.

10    David Wallace, director of counseling at the University of Central Florida, said teachers are paying closer attention to violent material in writing assignments—warning bells that had worried Cho's professors.

11    "Now people are wondering, 'Is this something that could be more ominous?'" he said. "Are we talking about the Stephen Kings of the future or about somebody who's seriously thinking about doing something harmful?"

12    The downside is officials may be hypersensitive to any eccentricity. Says Susan Davis, an attorney who works in student affairs at the University of Virginia: "There's no question there's some hysteria and there's some things we don't need to see."

13    Changes are being made to privacy policies. In Virginia, a measure signed into law Wednesday by Gov. Tim Kaine requires colleges to bring parents into the loop when dependent students may be a danger to themselves or others.

14    Even before Virginia Tech, Cornell University had begun treating students as dependents of their parents unless told otherwise—an

aggressive legal strategy that gives the school more leeway to contact parents with concerns without students' permission.

15    In Washington, meanwhile, federal officials are trying to clarify privacy guidelines so faculty won't hesitate to report potential threats.

16    "Nobody's throwing privacy out the window, but we are coming out of an era when individual rights were paramount on college campuses," said Brett Sokolow, who advises colleges on risk management. "What colleges are struggling with now is a better balance of those individual rights and community protections."

17    The big change since the Virginia Tech shootings, legal experts say, is colleges have shed some of their fear of violating the federal Family Educational Rights and Privacy Act.

18    Many faculty hadn't realized that the law applies only to educational records, not observations of classroom behavior, or that it contains numerous exceptions.

19    The stigma of mental illness, in some cases, has grown. "In general, the attention to campus mental health was desperately needed," said Alison Malmon, founder of the national Active Minds group. But some of the debate, she added, "has turned in a direction that does not necessarily support students."

20    All the talk of "threat assessments" and better-trained campus SWAT teams, she said, has distracted the public from the fact that the mentally ill rarely commit violence—especially against others.

21    "I know that, for many students, it made them feel more stigmatized," Malmon said. "It made them more likely to keep their mental health history silent."

22    Sokolow, the risk consultant for colleges, estimated in the aftermath of the Virginia Tech and NIU shootings, the schools he works with spent $25 on police and communications for every $1 on mental health. Only recently has he seen a shift.

23    "Campuses come to me, they want me to help them start behavioral intervention systems," Sokolow said. "Then they go to the president to get the money and, oh, well, the money went into the door locks."

24    Phone messaging systems and security are nice, he said, but "there is nothing about text-messaging that is going to prevent violence."

## The Family Educational Rights And Privacy Act

United States Code
Title 20. Education
CHAPTER 31. General Provisions
Concerning Education
§ 1232g. Family Educational
and Privacy Rights

*Following are excepts from the Family Educational Rights and Privacy Act (FERPA), the federal law enacted in 1974 that governs restrictions on the release of student educational records. FERPA provides for the withholding of federal funds to educational institutions that violate its provisions, and it is the federal guarantor of the privacy rights of post-secondary students.*

(1) (A) No funds shall be made available under any applicable program to any educational agency or institution which has a policy of denying, or which effectively prevents, the parents of students who are or have been in attendance at a school of such agency or at such institution, as the case may be, the right to inspect and review the education records of their children. If any material or document in the education record of a student includes information on more than one student, the parents of one of such students shall have the right to inspect and review only such part of such material or document as relates to such student or to be informed of the specific information contained in such part of such material. Each educational agency or institution shall establish appropriate procedures for the granting of a request by parents for access to the education records of their children within a reasonable period of time, but in no case more than forty-five days after the request has been made. . . .

(C) The first sentence of subparagraph (A) shall not operate to make available to students in institutions of postsecondary education the following materials:

        (i)  financial records of the parents of the student or any information contained therein;

(ii)  confidential letters and statements of recommenda-
tion, which were placed in the education records
prior to January 1, 1975, if such letters or statements
are not used for purposes other than those for which
they were specifically intended;

(iii)  if the student has signed a waiver of the student's right
of access under this subsection in accordance with
subparagraph (D), confidential recommendations—

  (I)  respecting admission to any educational agency
or institution,

  (II)  respecting an application for employment, and

  (III)  respecting the receipt of an honor or honorary
recognition.

. . . . . . . . . . . . . . . . . . . . . . . . . . . . . . . . . . . . . . . . . . . . . . . . . . .

(B) The term "education records" does not include—

(i)  records of instructional, supervisory, and administra-
tive personnel and educational personnel ancillary
thereto which are in the sole possession of the
maker thereof and which are not accessible or
revealed to any other person except a substitute;

(ii)  records maintained by a law enforcement unit of the
educational agency or institution that were created by
that law enforcement unit for the purpose of law
enforcement;

(iii)  in the case of persons who are employed by an educational agency or institution but who are not in
attendance at such agency or institution, records
made and maintained in the normal course of business which relate exclusively to such person in that
person's capacity as an employee and are not available for use for any other purpose; or

(iv)  records on a student who is eighteen years of age or
older, or is attending an institution of postsecondary
education, which are made or maintained by a physician, psychiatrist, psychologist, or other recognized
professional or paraprofessional acting in his professional or paraprofessional capacity, or assisting in that

capacity, and which are made, maintained, or used only in connection with the provision of treatment to the student, and are not available to anyone other than persons providing such treatment, except that such records can be personally reviewed by a physician or other appropriate professional of the student's choice. . . .

(h) Certain disciplinary action information allowable. Nothing in this section shall prohibit an educational agency or institution from—

(1)   including appropriate information in the education record of any student concerning disciplinary action taken against such student for conduct that posed a significant risk to the safety or well-being of that student, other students, or other members of the school community; or

(2)   disclosing such information to teachers and school officials, including teachers and school officials in other schools, who have legitimate educational interests in the behavior of the student.

## Consider Your Purpose

Your specific purpose in writing an argument synthesis is crucial. What exactly you want to do will affect your claim and the way you organize the evidence. Your purpose may be clear to you before you begin research, or it may not emerge until after you have completed your research. Of course, the sooner your purpose is clear to you, the fewer wasted motions you will make. On the other hand, the more you approach research as an exploratory process, the likelier that your conclusions will emerge from the sources themselves rather than from preconceived ideas. Each new writing project will have its rhythm in this regard. Be flexible in your approach: through some combination of preconceived structures and invigorating discoveries, you will find your way to the source materials that will yield a promising paper.

Let's say that while reading these three (and additional) sources on the debate about campus safety and student privacy you shared the outrage of many who blamed the university and the federal privacy laws on which they relied for not using the available information in a way that might have helped spare the lives of those who died. Perhaps you also blamed the legislators who wrote the privacy laws for being more concerned about the confidentiality of the mental health records of the individual person than with the privacy of the larger college population. Perhaps, you concluded, society has gone too far in valuing privacy more than it appears to value safety.

On the other hand, in your own role as a student, perhaps you share the high value placed on the privacy of sensitive information about yourself. After all, one of the functions of higher education is to foster students' independence as they make the transition from adolescence to adulthood. You can understand that many students like yourself might not want parents or others to know details about academic records or disciplinary measures, much less information about therapy sought and undertaken at school. Historically, in the decades since the university officially stood *in loco parentis*—in place of parents—students have struggled hard to win the same civil liberties and rights (including the right to privacy) of their elders.

Further, you may wonder whether federal privacy laws do in fact forbid the sharing of information about potentially dangerous students when the health and safety of others are at stake. A little research may begin to confirm your doubts about whether Virginia Tech officials were as helpless as they claim they were.

Your purpose in writing, then, emerges from these kinds of responses to the source materials you find.

## Making a Claim: Formulate a Thesis

As we indicated in the introduction to this chapter, one useful way of approaching an argument is to see it as making a *claim*. A claim is a proposition, a conclusion that you have made, that you are trying to prove or demonstrate. If your purpose is to argue that we should work to ensure campus safety without enacting restrictive laws that overturn the hard-won privacy rights of students, then that claim (generally expressed in one-sentence form as a *thesis*) is at the heart of your argument.

You will draw support from your sources as you argue logically for your claim.

Not every piece of information in a source is useful for supporting a claim. You must read with care and select the opinions, facts, and statistics that best advance your position. You may even find yourself drawing support from sources that make claims entirely different from your own. For example, in researching the subject of student privacy and campus safety, you may come across editorials arguing that in the wake of the Virginia Tech shootings student privacy rights should be greatly restricted. Perhaps you will find information in these sources to help support your own contrary arguments.

You might use one source as part of a *counterargument*—an argument opposing your own—so you can demonstrate its weaknesses and, in the process, strengthen your own claim. On the other hand, the author of one of your sources may be so convincing in supporting a claim that you will adopt it yourself, either partially or entirely. The point is that *the argument is in your hands*. You must devise it yourself and use your sources in ways that will support the claim you present in your thesis.

You may not want to divulge your thesis until the end of the paper, thereby drawing the reader along toward your conclusion, allowing that thesis to flow naturally out of the argument and the evidence on which it is based. If you do this, you are working *inductively*. Or you may wish to be more direct and (after an introduction) *begin* with your thesis, following the thesis statement with evidence and reasoning to support it. If you do this, you are working *deductively*. In academic papers, deductive arguments are far more common than inductive ones.

Based on your reactions to reading sources—and perhaps also on your own inclinations as a student—you may find yourself essentially in sympathy with the approach to privacy taken by one of the schools covered in your sources, M.I.T. At the same time, you may feel that M.I.T.'s position does not demonstrate sufficient concern for campus safety and that Cornell's position, on the other hand, restricts student privacy too much. Perhaps most important, you conclude that we don't need to change the law because, if correctly interpreted, the law already incorporates a good balance between privacy and safety. After a few tries, you develop the following thesis:

> In responding to the Virginia Tech killings, we should resist rolling back federal rules protecting student privacy; for as long as college officials effectively respond to signs of trouble, these rules already provide a workable balance between privacy and public safety.

## Decide How You Will Use Your Source Material

Your claim commits you to (1) arguing that student privacy should remain protected, and (2) demonstrating that federal law already strikes a balance between privacy and public safety. The sources (some provided here, some located elsewhere) offer information and ideas—evidence—that will allow you to support your claim. The excerpt from the official report on the Virginia Tech shootings reveals a finding that school officials failed to correctly interpret federal privacy rules and failed to "intervene effectively." The article "Virginia Tech Massacre Has Altered Campus Mental Health Systems" outlines some of the ways that campuses around the country have instituted policy changes regarding troubled students and privacy in the wake of Virginia Tech. And the excerpt from the Family Educational Rights and Privacy Act (FERPA), the federal law, reveals that restrictions on revealing students' confidential information have a crucial exception for "the health or safety of the student or other person." (Note that that these and other sources not included in this chapter will be cited in the example paper.)

## Develop an Organizational Plan

Having established your overall purpose and your claim, having developed a thesis (which may change as you write and revise the paper), and having decided how to draw upon your source materials, how do you logically organize your paper? In many cases, a well-written thesis will suggest an organization. Thus, the first part of your paper will deal with the debate over rolling back student privacy. The second part will argue that as long as educational institutions behave proactively—that is, as long as they actively seek to help troubled students and foster campus safety—existing federal rules already preserve a balance between privacy and safety. Sorting through your material and categorizing it by topic and subtopic, you might compose the following outline:

I. Introduction. Recap Va. Tech shooting. College officials, citing privacy rules, did not act on available info about shooter with history of mental problems.

II. Federal rules on privacy. Subsequent debate over balance between privacy and campus safety. Pendulum now moving back toward safety. <u>Thesis</u>.

III. Developments in student privacy in recent decades.

    A. Doctrine of <u>in loco parentis</u> defines college-student relationship.

    B. Movement away from <u>in loco parentis</u> begins in 1960s, in context not only of student rights but also broader civil rights struggles of the period.

    C. FERPA, enacted 1974, establishes new federal rules protecting student privacy.

IV. Arguments <u>against</u> student privacy.

    A. In wake of Virginia Tech, many blame FERPA protections and college officials, believing privacy rights have been taken too far, putting campus community at risk.

    B. Cornell rolls back some FERPA privacy rights.

V. Arguments <u>for</u> student privacy.

    A. M.I.T. strongly defends right to privacy.

    B. Problem is not federal law but incorrect interpretation of federal law. FERPA provides health and safety exceptions. Virginia Tech officials erred in citing FERPA for not sharing info about shooter earlier.

C. Univ. of Kentucky offers good balance between competing claims of privacy and safety.
1. watch lists of troubled students
2. threat assessment groups
3. open communication among university officials

VI. Conclusion.

A. Virginia Tech incident was tragic but should not cause us to overturn hard-won privacy rights.

B. We should support a more pro-active approach to student mental health problems and improve communication between departments.

## Formulate an Argument Strategy

The argument that emerges through this outline will build not only on evidence drawn from sources but also on the writer's assumptions. Consider the bare-bones logic of the argument:

Laws protecting student privacy serve a good purpose. (*assumption*)

If properly interpreted and implemented, federal law as currently written is sufficient both to protect student privacy and to ensure campus safety. (*support*)

We should not change federal law to overturn or restrict student privacy rights. (*claim*)

The crucial point about which reasonable people will disagree is the *assumption* that laws protecting student privacy serve a good purpose. Those who wish to restrict the information made available to parents are likely to agree with this assumption. Those who favor a policy that allows college officials to inform parents of problems without their children's permission are likely to disagree.

Writers can accept or partially accept an opposing assumption by making a *concession*, in the process establishing themselves as reasonable and willing to compromise (see pp. 126–127). David Harrison does exactly this in the model synthesis that follows when he summarizes the policies of the University of Kentucky. By raising objections to his own position and conceding some validity to them, he blunts the effectiveness of *counterarguments*. Thus, Harrison concedes the absolute requirement for campus safety, but he argues that this requirement can be satisfied as long as campus officials correctly interpret existing federal law and implement proactive procedures aimed at dealing more effectively with troubled students.

The *claim* of the example argument about privacy vs. safety is primarily a claim about *policy*, about actions that should (or should not) be taken. An argument can also concern a claim about *facts* (Does X exist? How can we define X? Does X lead to Y?), a claim about *value* (What is X worth?), or a claim about *cause and effect* (Why did X happen?). The present argument rests to some degree on a dispute about cause and effect. No one disputes that the primary cause of this tragedy was that a disturbed student was not stopped before he killed people. But many have disputed the secondary cause: Did the massacre happen, in part, because federal law prevented officials from sharing crucial information about the disturbed student? Or did it happen, in part, because university officials failed to interpret correctly what they could and could not do under the law? As you read the following paper, observe how these opposing views are woven into the argument.

## Draft and Revise Your Synthesis

The final draft of a completed synthesis, based on the outline above, follows. **Thesis, transitions, and topic sentences are highlighted;** Modern Language Association (MLA) documentation style is used throughout (except in the citing of federal law).

*A cautionary note:* When writing syntheses, it is all too easy to become careless in properly crediting your sources. Before drafting your paper, always review the section on "Avoiding Plagiarism" (pp. 34–36).

## MODEL ARGUMENT SYNTHESIS

Harrison 1

David Harrison
Professor Shanker
Law and Society I
14 February 2009

Balancing Privacy and Safety
in the Wake of Virginia Tech

1    On April 16, 2007, Seung Hui Cho, a mentally ill
student at Virginia Polytechnic Institute, shot to death
32 fellow students and faculty members, and injured
17 others, before killing himself. It was the worst mass
shooting in U.S. history, and the fact that it took place on
a college campus lent a special horror to the event. In the
days after the tragedy, several facts about Seung Hui Cho
came to light. According to the official Virginia State
Panel report on the killings, Cho had exhibited signs of
mental disturbance, including "suicidal and homicidal
ideations" dating back to high school. And during Cho's
junior year at Virginia Tech, numerous incidents occurred
that provided clear warnings of Cho's mental instability
and violent impulses (Virginia Tech Review 1).
University administrators, faculty, and officials were
aware of these incidents but failed to intervene to prevent
the impending tragedy.

2    In the search for answers, attention quickly focused on
federal rules governing student privacy that Virginia Tech
officials said prevented them from communicating effectively
with each other or with Cho's parents regarding his troubles.

These rules, the officials argued, prohibit the sharing of information concerning students' mental health with parents or other students. The publicity about such restrictions revived an ongoing debate over university policies that balance student privacy against campus safety. In the wake of the Virginia Tech tragedy, the pendulum seems to have swung in favor of safety. In April 2008, Virginia Governor Tim Kaine signed into law a measure requiring colleges to alert parents when dependent students may be a danger to themselves or to others ("Virginia Tech Massacre" 1). Peter Lake, an educator at Stetson University College of Law, predicted that in the wake of Virginia Tech, "people will go in a direction of safety over privacy" (qtd. in Bernstein, "Mother").

3

   The shootings at Virginia Tech demonstrate, in the most horrifying way, the need for secure college campuses. Nevertheless, privacy remains a crucial right to most Americans--including college students, many of whom for the first time are exercising their prerogatives as adults. Many students who pose no threat to anyone will, and should, object strenuously to university administrators peering into and making judgments about their private lives. Some might be unwilling to seek professional therapy if they know that the records of their counseling sessions might be released to their parents or to other students. In responding to the Virginia Tech killings, we should resist rolling back federal rules protecting student privacy; for as long as college officials effectively respond to signs of trouble, these rules already provide a workable balance between privacy and public safety.

4    In these days of Facebook and reality TV, the notion of privacy rights, particularly for young people, may seem quaint. In fact, recently a top lawyer for the search engine Google claimed that in the Internet age, young people just don't care about privacy the way they once did (Cohen A17). Whatever the changing views of privacy in a wired world, the issue of student privacy rights is a serious legal matter that must be seen in the context of the student-college relationship, which has its historical roots in the doctrine of in loco parentis, Latin for "in the place of the parents." Generally, this doctrine is understood to mean that the college stands in place as the student's parent or guardian. The college therefore has "a duty to protect the safety, morals, and welfare of their students, just as parents are expected to protect their children" (Pollet).

5    Writing of life at the University of Michigan before the 1960s, one historian observes that "in loco parentis comprised an elaborate structure of written rules and quiet understandings enforced in the trenches by housemothers [who] governed much of the what, where, when, and whom of students' lives, especially women: what to wear to dinner, what time to be home, where, when, and for how long they might receive visitors" (Tobin).

6    During the 1960s court decisions began to chip away at the doctrine of in loco parentis. These rulings illustrate that the students' rights movement during that era was an integral part of a broader contemporary social movement for civil rights and liberties. In Dixon v. Alabama State Board of Education, Alabama State College invoked in loco parentis to defend its decision to expel six African-American students

Harrison 4

without due process for participating in a lunchroom
counter sit-in. Eventually, a federal appeals court rejected
the school's claim to unrestrained power, ruling that students'
constitutional rights did not end once they stepped onto
campus (Weigel).

7  Students were not just fighting for the right to hold
hands in dorm rooms; they were also asserting their
rights as the vanguard of a social revolution. As Stetson
law professor Robert Bickel notes: "The fall of in loco
parentis in the 1960s correlated exactly with the rise of
student economic power and the rise of student civil
rights" (qtd. in Weigel).

8  The students' rights movement received a further boost
with the Family Educational Rights and Privacy Act
(FERPA), signed into law by President Ford in 1974.
FERPA barred schools from releasing educational
records--including mental health records--without the student's permission. The Act provides some
important exceptions: educational records can be
released in the case of health and safety emergencies or
if the student is declared a dependent on his or her
parents' tax returns (Federal).

9  In the wake of Virginia Tech, however, many observers
pointed the finger of blame at federal restrictions on sharing
available mental health information. Also held responsible
were the school's officials, who admitted knowing of Cho's
mental instability but claimed that FERPA prevented them
from doing anything about it. The State of Virginia official
report on the killings notes as follows:

University officials . . . explained their failures to communicate with one another or with Cho's parents by
noting their belief that such communications are prohibited by the federal laws governing the privacy of
health and education records. (Virginia Tech Review 2)

10    Observers were quick to declare the system broken.
"Laws Limit Schools Even after Alarms," trumpeted a
headline in the Philadelphia Inquirer (Gammage and
Burling). Commentators attacked federal privacy law,
charging that the pendulum had swung too far away from
campus safety. Judging from this letter to the editor of the
Wall Street Journal, many agreed wholeheartedly:

Parents have a right to know if their child has a serious problem, and they need to know the progress of
their child's schoolwork, especially if they are paying
the cost of the education. Anything less than this is
criminal. (Guerriero)

11    As part of this public clamor, some schools have enacted
policies that effectively curtail student privacy in favor of
campus safety. For example: after Virginia Tech, Cornell
University began assuming that students were dependents of their parents. Exploiting what the Wall Street
Journal termed a "rarely used legal exception" in FERPA
allows Cornell to provide parents with confidential
information without students' permission (Bernstein,
"Bucking" A9).

12    Conversely, the Massachusetts Institute of Technology
lies at the opposite end of the spectrum from Cornell in its
staunch defense of student privacy. MIT has stuck to its
position even in the wake of Virginia Tech, recently

demanding that the mother of a missing MIT student obtain
a subpoena in order to access his dorm room and e-mail
records. That student was later found dead, an apparent
suicide (Bernstein, "Mother"). Even in the face of lawsuits,
MIT remains committed to its stance. Its Chancellor
explained the school's position this way:

> Privacy is important. . . . Different students will do
> different things they absolutely don't want their par-
> ents to know about. . . . Students expect this kind of
> safe place where they can address their difficulties,
> try out lifestyles, and be independent of their parents
> (qtd. in Bernstein, "Mother").

13    One can easily understand how parents would be outraged by the MIT position. No parent would willingly let
his or her child enter an environment where that child's
safety cannot be assured. Just as the first priority for any
government is to protect its citizens, the first priority of an
educational institution must be to keep its students safe.
But does this responsibility justify rolling back student
privacy rights or returning to a more traditional interpretation
of in loco parentis in the relationship between a university
and its students? No, for the simple reason that the choice is
a false one.

14    As long as federal privacy laws are properly interpreted
and implemented, they do nothing to endanger campus
safety. The problem at Virginia Tech was not the federal
government's policy; it was the university's own practices
based on a faulty interpretation of that policy. The breakdown began with the failure of Virginia Tech officials
to understand federal privacy laws. Interpreted correctly,

these laws would <u>not</u> have prohibited officials from notifying appropriate authorities of Cho's problems. The Virginia Tech Review Panel report was very clear on this point: "[F]ederal laws and their state counterparts afford ample leeway to share information in potentially dangerous situations" (2). FERPA does, in fact, provide for a "health and safety emergencies" exception; educational records <u>can</u> be released without the student's consent "in connection with an emergency, [to] appropriate persons if the knowledge of such information is necessary to protect the health or safety of the student or other person . . . " (232g (b) (1) (g-h)). But Virginia Tech administrators did not invoke this important exception to FERPA's privacy rules.

15    An editorial in the <u>Christian Science Monitor</u> suggested several other steps that the university legally could have taken, including informing Cho's parents that he had been briefly committed to a mental health facility, a fact that was public information. The editorial concluded, scornfully, that "federal law, at least, does recognize a balance between privacy and public safety, even when colleges can't, or won't" ("Perilous").

16    To be fair, such confusion about FERPA's contingencies appears widespread among college officials. For this reason, the U. S. Department of Education's Department's revised privacy regulations, announced in March 2008 and intended to "clarify" when schools may release student records, are welcome and necessary. But simply reassuring anxious university officials that they won't lose federal funds for revealing confidential

student records won't be enough to ensure campus safety. We need far more effective intervention for troubled students than the kind provided by Virginia Tech, which the Virginia Tech Review Panel blasted for its "lack of resources" and "passivity" (2).

17    Schools like the University of Kentucky offer a positive example of such intervention, demonstrating that colleges can adopt a robust approach to student mental health without infringing on privacy rights. At Kentucky, "threat assessment groups" meet regularly to discuss a "watch list" of troubled students and decide what to do about them (McMurray). These committees emphasize proactiveness and communication--elements that were sorely missing at Virginia Tech. The approach represents a prudent middle ground between the extreme positions of MIT and Cornell.

18    Schools such as Kentucky carry out their policies with a firm eye towards student privacy rights. For example, the University of Kentucky's director of counseling attends the threat assessment group's meetings but draws a clear line at what information she can share--for instance, whether or not a student has been undergoing counseling. Instead, the group looks for other potential red flags, such as a sharp drop-off in grades or difficulty functioning in the campus environment (McMurray). This open communication between university officials presumably will also help with delicate judgments--whether, for example, a student's violent story written for a creative writing class is an indication of mental instability or simply an early work by the next Stephen King ("Virginia Tech Massacre" 1).

19    What happened at Virginia Tech was a tragedy. Few of us can appreciate the grief of the parents of the shooting victims at Virginia Tech, parents who trusted that their children would be safe and who were devastated when that faith was betrayed. To these parents, the words of the MIT chancellor quoted earlier--platitudes about students "try[ing] out lifestyles" or "address[ing] their difficulties"--must sound hollow. But we must guard against allowing a few isolated incidents, however tragic, to restrict the rights of millions of students, the vast majority of whom graduate college safely and without incident. Schools must not use Virginia Tech as a pretext to bring back the bad old days of resident assistants snooping on the private lives of students and infringing on their privacy. That step is the first down a slippery slope of dictating morality. Both the federal courts and Congress have rejected that approach and for good reason have established the importance of privacy rights on campus. These rights must be preserved.

20    The Virginia Tech shooting does not demonstrate a failure of current policy, but rather a breakdown in the enforcement of policy. In its wake, universities have undertaken important modifications to their procedures. We should support changes that involve a more proactive approach to student mental health and improvements in communication between departments, such as those at the University of Kentucky. Such measures will not only bring confidential help to the troubled students who need it, they will also improve the safety of the larger college community. At the same time, these measures will preserve hard-won privacy rights on campus.

Works Cited

Bernstein, Elizabeth. "Bucking Privacy Concerns, Cornell Acts as Watchdog." Wall Street Journal 27 Dec. 2007: A1+.

---. "A Mother Takes On MIT." Wall Street Journal 20 Sept. 2007: A1.

Cohen, Adam. "One Friend Facebook Hasn't Made Yet: Privacy Rights." New York Times 18 Feb. 2008: A1+.

Federal Educational Rights and Privacy Act (FERPA). 20 U.S.C. §1232g (b) (1) (g–h) (2006).

Gammage, Jeff, and Stacy Burling. "Laws Limit Schools Even after Alarms." Philadelphia Inquirer 19 Apr. 2007: A1.

Guerriero, Dom. Letter. Wall Street Journal 7 Jan. 2008.

McMurray, Jeffrey. "Colleges Are Watching Troubled Students." AP Online 28 Mar. 2008. 5 May 2008 <http://www.wtopnews.com/ ?nid=104&pid=0&sid=1374703&page=1>.

"Perilous Privacy at Virginia Tech." Editorial. Christian Science Monitor 4 Sept. 2007: 8.

Pollet, Susan J. "Is 'In Loco Parentis' at the College Level a Dead Doctrine?" New York Law Journal 288 (2002): 4.

Tobin, James. "The Day 'In Loco Parentis' Died." Michigan Today Nov. 2007. 5 May 2008 <http://michigantoday/ umich.edu/2007/nov/dorms.php>.

"Virginia Tech Massacre Has Altered Campus Mental Health Systems." Los Angeles Times 14 Apr. 2008: A1+.

Virginia Tech Review Panel. Mass Shootings at Virginia Tech, April 16, 2007: Report of the Virginia Tech

Harrison 11

Review Panel Presented to Timothy M. Kaine,
Governor, Commonwealth of Virginia. Aug. 2007.
Weigel, David. "Welcome to the Fun-Free University:
The Return of In Loco Parentis Is Killing Student
Freedom." Reason Oct. 2004. 5 May 2008
<http://www.reason.com/news/show/29271.html>.

## The Strategy of the Argument Synthesis

In his argument synthesis, Harrison attempts to support a
*claim*—one that favors laws protecting student privacy while at
the same time helping to ensure campus safety—by offering
*support* in the form of facts (what campuses such as the
University of Kentucky are doing, what Virginia Tech officials
did and failed to do) and opinions (testimony of persons on both
sides of the issue). However, because Harrison's claim rests
upon an *assumption* about the value of student privacy laws, its
effectiveness depends partially upon the extent to which we, as
readers, agree with this assumption. (See our discussion of
assumptions in Chapter 2, pp. 55–57.) An assumption (sometimes called a warrant) is a generalization or principle about
how the world works or should work—a fundamental statement of belief about facts or values. In this case, the underlying
assumption is that college students, as emerging adults, and as
citizens with civil rights, are entitled to keep their educational
records private. Harrison makes this assumption explicit.
Though you are under no obligation to do so, stating assumptions explicitly will clarify your arguments to readers.

Assumptions are often deeply rooted in people's psyches,
sometimes derived from lifelong experiences and observations
and not easily changed, even by the most logical of arguments.
People who lost loved ones in incidents such as Virginia Tech,

or people who believe that the right to safety of the larger campus community outweighs the right of individual student privacy, are not likely to accept the assumption underlying this paper, nor are they likely to accept the support provided by Harrison. But readers with no firm opinion might well be persuaded and could come to agree with him that existing federal law protecting student privacy is sufficient to protect campus safety, provided that campus officials act responsibly.

A discussion of the model argument's paragraphs, along with the argument strategy for each, follows. Note that the paper devotes one paragraph to developing each section of the outline on pp. 102–103. Note also that Harrison avoids plagiarism by the careful attribution and quotation of sources.

- **Paragraph 1:** Harrison summarizes the key events of the Virginia Tech killings and establishes that Cho's mental instability was previously known to university officials.

  **Argument strategy:** Opening with the bare facts of the massacre, Harrison proceeds to lay the basis for the reaction against privacy rules that will be described in the paragraphs to follow. To some extent, Harrison encourages the reader to share the outrage by many in the general public that university officials failed to act to prevent the killings before they started.

- **Paragraph 2:** Harrison now explains the federal rules governing student privacy and discusses the public backlash against such rules and the new law signed by the governor of Virginia restricting privacy at colleges within the state.

  **Argument strategy:** This paragraph highlights the debate over student privacy—and in particular the sometimes conflicting demands of student privacy and campus safety that will be central to the rest of the paper. Harrison cites both fact (the new Virginia law) and opinion (the quotation by Peter Lake) to develop this paragraph.

- **Paragraph 3:** Harrison further clarifies the two sides of the apparent conflict between privacy and safety, maintaining that both represent important social values but concluding with a thesis that argues for not restricting privacy.

  **Argument strategy:** For the first time, Harrison reveals his own position on the issue. He begins the paragraph by conceding the need for secure campuses but begins to make the case for privacy (for example, without privacy rules students might be reluctant to enter therapy). In his thesis he emphasizes that the demands of both privacy and safety can be satisfied because existing federal rules incorporate the necessary balance.

- **Paragraphs 4–7:** Paragraphs 4–7 constitute the next section of the paper (see outline, pp. 102–103), covering the developments in student privacy over the past few decades. Paragraphs 4 and 5 treat the doctrine of *in loco parentis*; paragraph 6 discusses how court decisions like *Dixon v. Alabama State Board of Education* began to erode this doctrine.

  **Argument strategy:** This section of the paper establishes the situation that existed on college campuses before the 1960s—and presumably would exist again were privacy laws to be rolled back. By linking the erosion of the *in loco parentis* doctrine to the civil rights struggle, Harrison attempts to bestow upon pre-1960s college students (especially women), who were "parented" by college administrators, something of the ethos of African-Americans fighting for full citizenship during the civil rights era. Essentially, Harrison is making an analogy between the two groups—one that readers may or may not accept.

- **Paragraph 8:** This paragraph on FERPA constitutes the final part of the section of the paper dealing with the evolution of student privacy since before the 1960s. Harrison explains what FERPA is and introduces an exception to its privacy rules that will be more fully developed later in the paper.

**Argument strategy:** FERPA is the federal law central to the debate over the balance between privacy and safety, so Harrison introduces it here as the culmination of a series of developments that weakened *in loco parentis* and guaranteed a certain level of student privacy. But since Harrison in his thesis argues that federal law on student privacy already establishes a balance between privacy and safety, he ends the paragraph by referring to the "health and safety" exception, an exception that will become important later in his argument.

- **Paragraphs 9–11:** These paragraphs constitute the section of the paper that covers the arguments **against** student privacy. Paragraph 9 treats public reaction against both FERPA and Virginia Tech officials who were accused of being more concerned with privacy than with safety. Paragraph 10 cites anti-privacy sentiments expressed in newspapers. Paragraph 11 explains how, in the wake of Virginia Tech, schools like Cornell have enacted new policies restricting student privacy.

  **Argument strategy:** Harrison sufficiently respects the sentiments of those whose position he opposes to deal at some length with the counterarguments to his thesis. He quotes the official report on the mass shootings to establish that Virginia Tech officials believed that they were acting according to the law. He quotes the writer of an angry letter about parents' right to know without attempting to rebut its arguments. In outlining the newly restrictive Cornell policies on privacy, Harrison also establishes what he considers an extreme reaction to the massacres: essentially gutting student privacy rules. He is therefore setting up one position on the debate which will later be contrasted with other positions—those of M.I.T. and the University of Kentucky.

- **Paragraphs 12–18:** These paragraphs constitute the section of the paper devoted to arguments **for** student privacy. Paragraphs 12 and 13 discuss the M.I.T. position on privacy, as expressed by its chancellor. Paragraph 14 refocuses on FERPA and quotes language to demonstrate that existing federal law provides a health and safety exception to the enforcement of privacy rules. Paragraph 15 quotes an editorial supporting this interpretation of FERPA. Paragraph 16 concedes the existence of confusion about federal rules and makes the transition to an argument about the need for more effective action by campus officials to prevent tragedies like this one.

**Argument strategy:** Since these paragraphs express Harrison's position, as embedded in his thesis, this is the longest segment of the discussion. Paragraphs 12 and 13 discuss the M.I.T. position on student privacy, which (given that school's failure to accommodate even prudent demands for safety) Harrison believes is too extreme. Notice the transition at the end of paragraph: conceding that colleges have a responsibility to keep students safe, Harrison poses a question: Does the goal of keeping students safe justify the rolling back of privacy rights? In a pivotal sentence, he responds, "No, for the simple reason that the choice is a false one." Paragraph 14 develops this response and presents the heart of Harrison's argument. Recalling the health and safety exception introduced in paragraph 9, Harrison now explains *why* the choice is false: he quotes the exact language of FERPA to establish that the problem at Virginia Tech was not due to federal law that prevented campus officials from protecting students, but rather to campus officials who *misunderstood* the law. Paragraph 15 amplifies Harrison's argument with a reference to an editorial in the *Christian Science Monitor*. Paragraph 16 marks a transition, within this section, to a position (developed in paragraphs 17 and 18) that Harrison believes represents a sensible stance in the debate over campus safety and student privacy. Harrison bolsters his case by citing here, as elsewhere in the paper, the official report on the Virginia Tech killings. The report, prepared by an expert panel that devoted months to investigating the incident, carries considerable weight as evidence in this argument.

- **Paragraphs 17–18:** These paragraphs continue the arguments in favor of Harrison's position. They focus on new policies in practice at the University of Kentucky that offer a "prudent middle ground" in the debate.

    **Argument strategy:** Having discussed schools such as Cornell and M.I.T. where the reaction to the Virginia Tech killings was inadequate or unsatisfactory, Harrison now outlines a set of policies and procedures in place at the University of Kentucky since April 2007. Following the transition at the end of paragraph 16 on the need for more effective intervention on the part of campus officials, Harrison explains how Kentucky established a promising form of such intervention: watch lists of troubled students, threat assessment groups, and more open communication among university officials. Thus Harrison positions what is happening at the University of Kentucky—as opposed to rollbacks of federal rules—as the most effective way of preventing future killings like those at Virginia Tech. Kentucky therefore becomes a crucial example for Harrison of how to strike a good balance between the demands of student privacy and campus safety.

- **Paragraphs 19–20:** In his conclusion, Harrison reiterates points made in the body of the paper. In paragraph 19 he agrees that what happened at Virginia Tech was a tragedy but maintains that an isolated incident should not become an excuse for rolling back student privacy rights and bringing back "the bad old days" when campus officials took an active, and intrusive, interest in students' private lives. In paragraph 20, Harrison reiterates the position stated in his thesis: that the problem at Virginia Tech was not a restrictive federal policy that handcuffed administrators but a breakdown in enforcement. He concludes on a hopeful note that new policies established since Virginia Tech will both protect student privacy and improve campus safety.

**Argument strategy:** The last two paragraphs provide Harrison with a final opportunity for driving home his points. These two paragraphs to some degree parallel the structure of the thesis itself. In paragraph 19, Harrison makes a final appeal against rolling back student privacy rights. This appeal parallels the first clause of the thesis ("In responding to the Virginia Tech killings, we should resist rolling back federal rules protecting student privacy"). In paragraph 20, Harrison focuses not on federal law itself but rather on the kind of measures adopted by schools like the University of Kentucky that go beyond mere compliance with federal law—and thereby demonstrate the validity of part two of Harrison's thesis ("As long as college officials effectively respond to signs of trouble, these rules already provide a workable balance between privacy and public safety"). Harrison thus ends a paper on a grim subject with a note that provides some measure of optimism and that attempts to reconcile proponents on both sides of this emotional debate.

Another approach to an argument synthesis based on the same and additional sources could argue (along with some of the sources quoted in the model paper) that safety as a social value should never be outweighed by the right to privacy. Such a position could draw support from other practices in contemporary society—searches at airports, for example—illustrating that most people are willing to give up a certain measure of privacy, as well as convenience, in the interest of the safety of the community. Even if such an argument were not to call for a rollback of federal privacy rules, it could recommend modifying the language of the law to make doubly clear that safety trumps privacy. Some have even argued that safety would be improved if students and teachers were permitted to bring guns to campus and were thereby able to defend themselves and others in the event of being confronted by a deranged gunman. In the wake of Virginia Tech and other recent mass killings (such as the shooting deaths of five Amish children at their schoolhouse in 2006), it is difficult to conceive of support for an extreme claim that the rights of the individual are paramount and that privacy should always trump safety. A more reasonable argument might be made, working in counterpoint to the pro-privacy position of the M.I.T. chancellor, specifying more precisely the criteria that would constitute (in the language of FERPA) "significant risk to the safety or well-being" of the campus community. Having met the clearly defined threshold of a grave risk, university officials could then breach student privacy in the interest of the greater good.

Whatever your approach to a subject, in first *critically examining* the various sources and then *synthesizing* them to support a position about which you feel strongly, you are engaging in the kind of critical thinking that is essential to success in a good deal of academic and professional work.

---

### DEVELOPING AND ORGANIZING SUPPORT FOR YOUR ARGUMENTS

- *Summarize, paraphrase, and quote supporting evidence.* Draw upon the facts, ideas, and language in your sources.
- *Provide various types of evidence and motivational appeal.*
- *Use climactic order.* Save the most important evidence in support of your argument for the *end*, where it will have the most impact. Use the next most important evidence *first*.
- *Use logical or conventional order.* Use a form of organization appropriate to the topic, such as problem/solution; sides of a controversy; comparison/contrast; or a form of organization appropriate to the academic or professional discipline, such as a report of an experiment or a business plan.

*(Continued on next page)*

- *Present and respond to counterarguments.* Anticipate and evaluate arguments against your position.
- *Use concession.* Concede that one or more arguments against your position have some validity; re-assert, nonetheless, that your argument is the stronger one.

## DEVELOPING AND ORGANIZING THE SUPPORT FOR YOUR ARGUMENTS

Experienced writers seem to have an intuitive sense of how to develop and present supporting evidence for their claims; this sense is developed through much hard work and practice. Less experienced writers wonder what to say first, and having decided on that, wonder what to say next. There is no single method of presentation. But the techniques of even the most experienced writers often boil down to a few tried and tested arrangements.

As we've seen in the model synthesis in this chapter, the key to devising effective arguments is to find and use those kinds of support that most persuasively strengthen your claim. Some writers categorize support into two broad types: *evidence* and *motivational appeals*. Evidence, in the form of facts, statistics, and expert testimony, helps make the appeal to reason. Motivational appeals—appeals grounded in emotion and upon the authority of the speaker—are employed to get people to change their minds, to agree with the writer or speaker, or to decide upon a plan of activity.

Following are some of the most common strategies for using and organizing support for your claims.

### Summarize, Paraphrase, and Quote Supporting Evidence

In most of the papers and reports you will write in college and in the professional world, evidence and motivational appeals derive from your summarizing, paraphrasing, and quoting of material in sources that either have been provided to you or that you have independently researched. For example, in paragraph 9 of the model argument synthesis, Harrison uses a block quotation from the Virginia Tech Review Panel report to make the point that college officials believed they were prohibited by federal privacy law from communicating with one another about disturbed students like Cho. You will find another block quotation later in the synthesis and a number of brief quotations woven into sentences throughout. In addition, you will find summaries and paraphrases. In each case, Harrison is careful to cite sources.

## Provide Various Types of Evidence and Motivational Appeals

Keep in mind that you can use appeals to both reason and emotion. The appeal to reason is based on evidence that consists of a combination of *facts* and *expert testimony*. The sources by Tobin and Weigel, for example, offer facts about the evolution over the past few decades of the *in loco parentis* doctrine. Bernstein and McMurray interview college administrators at Cornell, M.I.T., and the University of Kentucky who explain the changing policies at those institutions. The model synthesis makes an appeal to emotion by engaging the reader's self-interest: If campuses are to be made more secure from the acts of mentally disturbed persons, then college officials should take a proactive approach to monitoring and intervention.

## Use Climactic Order

Climactic order is the arrangement of examples or evidence in order of anticipated impact on the reader, least to greatest. Organize by climactic order when you plan to offer a number of categories or elements of support for your claim. Recognize that some elements will be more important—and likely more persuasive—than others. The basic principle here is that you should *save the most important evidence for the end* because whatever you say last is what readers are likely to most remember best. A secondary principle is that whatever you say first is what they are *next* most likely to remember. Therefore, when you have several reasons to offer in support of your claim, an effective argument strategy is to present the second most important, then one or more additional reasons, and finally the most important reason. Paragraphs 7–11 of the model synthesis do exactly this.

## Use Logical or Conventional Order

Using logical or conventional order involves using as a template a pre-established pattern or plan for arguing your case.

- One common pattern is describing or arguing a *problem/solution*. Using this pattern, you begin with an introduction in which you typically define the problem, perhaps explain its origins, then offer one or more solutions, then conclude.

- Another common pattern presents *two sides of a controversy*. Using this pattern, you introduce the controversy and (in an argument synthesis) your own point of view or claim, then you explain the other side's arguments, providing reasons why your point of view should prevail.

- A third common pattern is *comparison-and-contrast*. This pattern is so important that we will discuss it separately in the next section.

- The order in which you present elements of an argument is sometimes dictated by the conventions of the discipline in which you are writing. For example, lab reports and experiments in the sciences and social sciences often follow this pattern: *Opening* or *Introduction, Methods and Materials* [of the experiment or study], *Results, Discussion.* Legal arguments often follow the so-called IRAC format: *Issue, Rule, Application, Conclusion.*

## Present and Respond to Counterarguments

When developing arguments on a controversial topic, you can effectively use *counterargument* to help support your claims. When you use counterargument, you present an argument *against* your claim and then show that this argument is weak or flawed. The advantage of this technique is that you demonstrate that you are aware of the other side of the argument and that you are prepared to answer it.

Here is how a counterargument is typically developed:

I. Introduction and claim
II. Main opposing argument
III. Refutation of opposing argument
IV. Main positive argument

## Use Concession

Concession is a variation of counterargument. As in counterargument, you present an opposing viewpoint, but instead of dismissing that position you *concede* that it has some validity and even some appeal, although your own position is the more reasonable one. This concession bolsters your standing as a fair-minded person who is not blind to the virtues of the other side. In the model synthesis, Harrison acknowledges the grief and sense of betrayal of the parents of the students who were killed. He concedes that parents have a right to expect that "the first priority of an educational institution must be to keep students safe." But he insists that this goal of achieving campus safety can be accomplished without rolling back hard-won privacy rights.

Here is an outline for a more typical concession argument:

I. Introduction and claim
II. Important opposing argument
III. Concession that this argument has some validity
IV. Positive argument(s)

Sometimes, when you are developing a counterargument or concession argument, you may become convinced of the validity of the opposing point of view and change your own views. Don't be afraid of this happening. Writing is a tool for learning. To change your mind because of new evidence is a sign of flexibility and maturity, and your writing can only be the better for it.

## THE COMPARISON-AND-CONTRAST SYNTHESIS

A particularly important type of argument synthesis is built on patterns of comparison and contrast. Techniques of comparison and contrast enable you to examine two subjects (or sources) in terms of one another. When you compare, you consider *similarities*. When you contrast, you consider *differences*. By comparing and contrasting, you perform a multifaceted analysis that often suggests subtleties that otherwise might not have come to your (or your reader's) attention.

To organize a comparison-and-contrast argument, you must carefully read sources in order to discover *significant criteria for analysis*. A *criterion* is a specific point to which both of your authors refer and about which they may agree or disagree. (For example, in a comparative report on compact cars, criteria for *comparison and contrast* might be road handling, fuel economy, and comfort of ride.) The best criteria are those that allow you not only to account for obvious similarities and differences—those concerning the main aspects of your sources or subjects—but also to plumb deeper, exploring subtle yet significant comparisons and contrasts among details or subcomponents, which you can then relate to your overall thesis.

Note that comparison-and-contrast is frequently not an end in itself but serves some larger purpose. Thus, a comparison-and-contrast synthesis may be a component of a paper that is essentially a critique, an explanatory synthesis, an argument synthesis, or an analysis.

## Organizing Comparison-and-Contrast Syntheses

Two basic approaches to organizing a comparison-and-contrast synthesis are organization by *source* and organization by *criteria*.

### Organizing by Source or Subject

You can organize a comparative synthesis by first summarizing each of your sources or subjects and then discussing the significant similarities and differences between them. Having read the summaries and become familiar with the distinguishing features of each source, your readers will most likely be able to appreciate the more obvious similarities and differences. In the discussion, your task is to consider both the obvious and the subtle comparisons and contrasts, focusing on the most significant—that is, on those that most clearly support your thesis.

Organization by source or subject works best with passages that can be briefly summarized. If the summary of your source or subject becomes too long, your readers might have forgotten the points you made in the first summary when they are reading the second. A comparison-and-contrast synthesis organized by source or subject might proceed like this:

I. Introduce the paper; lead to thesis.

II. Summarize source/subject A by discussing its significant features.

III. Summarize source/subject B by discussing its significant features.

IV. Discuss in a paragraph (or two) the significant points of comparison and contrast between sources or subjects A and B. Alternatively, begin the comparison-contrast in Section III as you introduce source/subject B.

V. Conclude with a paragraph in which you summarize your points and, perhaps, raise and respond to pertinent questions.

*Organizing by Criteria*

Instead of summarizing entire sources one at a time with the intention of comparing them later, you could discuss two sources simultaneously, examining the views of each author point by point (criterion by criterion), comparing and contrasting these views in the process. The criterion approach is best used when you have a number of points to discuss or when passages or subjects are long and/or complex. A comparison-and-contrast synthesis organized by criteria might look like this:

I. Introduce the paper; lead to thesis.

II. Criterion 1

  A. Discuss what author #1 says about this point. Or present situation #1 in light of this point.

  B. Discuss what author #2 says about this point, comparing and contrasting #2's treatment of the point with #1's. Or present situation #2 in light of this point and explain its differences from situation #1.

III. Criterion 2

  A. Discuss what author #1 says about this point. Or present situation #1 in light of this point.

  B. Discuss what author #2 says about this point, comparing and contrasting #2's treatment of the point with #1's. Or present situation #2 in light of this point and explain its differences from situation #1.

And so on, proceeding criterion by criterion until you have completed your discussion. Be sure to arrange criteria with a clear method; knowing how the discussion of one criterion leads to the next will ensure smooth transitions throughout your paper. End by summarizing your key points and perhaps raising and responding to pertinent questions.

However you organize your comparison-and-contrast synthesis, keep in mind that comparing and contrasting are not ends in themselves. Your discussion should point to a conclusion, an answer to the question "So what—why bother to compare and contrast in the first place?" If your discussion is part of a larger synthesis, point to and support the larger claim. If you write a stand-alone comparison-and-contrast, though, you must by the final paragraph answer the "Why bother?" question. The model comparison-and-contrast synthesis that follows does exactly this.

## A Case for Comparison-and-Contrast: World War I and World War II

Let's see how the principles of comparison-and-contrast can be applied to a response to a final examination question in a course on modern history. Imagine that having attended classes involving lecture and discussion, and having read excerpts from John Keegan's *The First World War* and Tony Judt's *Postwar: A History of Europe Since 1945*, you were presented with this examination question:

> Based on your reading to date, compare and contrast the two World Wars in light of any four or five criteria you think significant. Once you have called careful attention to both similarities and differences, conclude with an observation. What have you learned? What can your comparative analysis teach us?

### Comparison-and-Contrast Organized by Criteria

Here is a plan for a response, essentially a comparison-contrast synthesis, organized by *criteria* and beginning with the thesis—and the *claim*.

> Thesis: In terms of the impact on cities and civilian populations, the military aspects of the two wars in Europe, and their aftermaths, the differences between World War I and World War II considerably outweigh the similarities.

I.   Introduction. World Wars I and II were the most devastating conflicts in history. <u>Thesis</u>

II.  Summary of main similarities: causes, countries involved, battlegrounds, global scope.

III. First major difference: Physical impact of war.

   A. WWI was fought mainly in rural battlegrounds.

   B. In WWII cities were destroyed.

IV.  Second major difference: Effect on civilians.

   A. WWI fighting primarily involved soldiers.

   B. WWII involved not only military but also massive noncombatant casualties: civilian populations were displaced, forced into slave labor, and exterminated.

V.   Third major difference: Combat operations.

   A. World War I, in its long middle phase, was characterized by trench warfare.

   B. During the middle phase of World War II there was no major military action in Nazi-occupied Western Europe.

VI.  Fourth major difference: Aftermath.

   A. Harsh war terms imposed on defeated Germany contributed significantly to the rise of Hitler and World War II.

   B. Victorious allies helped rebuild West Germany after World War II but allowed Soviets to take over Eastern Europe.

VII. Conclusion. Since the end of World War II, wars have been far smaller in scope and destructiveness, and warfare has expanded to involve stateless combatants committed to acts of terror.

The following comparison-and-contrast synthesis, organized by criteria, is written according to the preceding plan. (Thesis and topic sentences are highlighted.)

## MODEL EXAM RESPONSE

1    World War I (1914-18) and World War II (1939-45)
were the most catastrophic and destructive conflicts in
human history. For those who believed in the steady but
inevitable progress of civilization, it was impossible to
imagine that two wars in the first half of the twentieth century could reach levels of barbarity and horror that would
outstrip those of any previous era. Historians estimate that
more than 22 million people, soldiers and civilians, died in
World War I; they estimate that between 40 and 50 million
died in World War II. In many ways, these two conflicts
were similar: they were fought on many of the same
European and Russian battlegrounds, with more or less the
same countries on opposing sides. Even many of the same
people were involved: Winston Churchill and Adolf Hitler
figured in both wars. And the main outcome in each case
was the same: total defeat for Germany. However, in terms
of the impact on cities and civilian populations, the military
aspects of the two wars in Europe, and their aftermaths, the
differences between World Wars I and II considerably outweigh the similarities.

2    The similarities are clear enough. In fact, many
historians regard World War II as a continuation--after an
intermission of about twenty years--of World War I. One
of the main causes of each war was Germany's dissatisfac-
tion and frustration with what it perceived as its diminished place in the world. Hitler launched World War II
partly out of revenge for Germany's humiliating defeat in
World War I. In each conflict Germany and its allies (the

Central Powers in WWI, the Axis in WWII) went to war against France, Great Britain, Russia (the Soviet Union in WWII), and eventually, the United States. Though neither conflict included literally the entire world, the participation of countries not only in Europe but also in the Middle East, the Far East, and the Western hemisphere made both of these conflicts global in scope. And as indicated earlier, the number of casualties in each war was unprecedented in history, partly because modern technology had enabled the creation of deadlier weapons--including tanks, heavy artillery, and aircraft--than had ever been used in warfare.

3   Despite these similarities, the differences between the two world wars are considerably more significant. One of the most noticeable differences was the physical impact of each war in Europe and Russia--the western and eastern fronts. The physical destruction of World War I was confined largely to the battlefield. The combat took place almost entirely in the rural areas of Europe and Russia. No major cities were destroyed in the first war; cathedrals, museums, government buildings, urban houses and apartments were left untouched. During the second war, in contrast, almost no city or town of any size emerged unscathed. Rotterdam, Warsaw, London, Minsk, and--when the Allies began their counterattack--almost every major city in Germany and Japan, including Berlin and Tokyo, were flattened. Of course, the physical devastation of the cities created millions of refugees, a phenomenon never experienced in World War I.

4    The fact that World War II was fought in the cities as well as on the battlefields meant that the second war had a much greater impact on civilians than did the first war. With few exceptions, the civilians in Europe during WWI were not driven from their homes, forced into slave labor, starved, tortured, or systematically exterminated. But all of these crimes happened routinely during WWII. The Nazi occupation of Europe meant that the civilian population of France, Belgium, Norway, the Netherlands, and other con-quered lands, along with the industries, railroads, and farms of these countries, were put into the service of the Third Reich. Millions of people from conquered Europe--those who were not sent directly to the death camps--were forcibly transported to Germany and put to work in support of the war effort.

5    During both wars, the Germans were fighting on two fronts--the western front in Europe and the eastern front in Russia. But while both wars were characterized by intense military activity during their initial and final phases, the middle and longest phases--at least in Europe--differed considerably. The middle phase of the First World War was characterized by trench warfare, a relatively static form of military activity in which fronts seldom moved, or moved only a few hundred yards at a time, even after major battles. By contrast, in the years between the German conquest of most of Europe by early 1941 and the Allied invasion of Normandy in mid-1944, there was no major fighting in Nazi-occupied Western Europe. (The land battles then shifted to North Africa and the Soviet Union.)

6   And of course, the two world wars differed in their aftermaths. The most significant consequence of World War I was that the humiliating and costly war reparations imposed on the defeated Germany by the terms of the 1919 Treaty of Versailles made possible the rise of Hitler and thus led directly to World War II. In contrast, after the end of the Second World War in 1945, the Allies helped rebuild West Germany (the portion of a divided Germany which it controlled), transformed the new country into a democracy, and helped make it into one of the most thriving economies of the world. But perhaps the most significant difference in the aftermath of each war involved Russia. That country, in a considerably weakened state, pulled out of World War I a year before hostilities ended so that it could consolidate its 1917 Revolution. Russia then withdrew into itself and took no significant part in European affairs until the Nazi invasion of the Soviet Union in 1941. In contrast, it was the Red Army in World War II that was most responsible for the crushing defeat of Germany. In recognition of its efforts and of its enormous sacrifices, the Allies allowed the Soviet Union to take control of the countries of Eastern Europe after the war, leading to fifty years of totalitarian rule--and the Cold War.

7   While the two world wars that devastated much of Europe were similar in that, at least according to some historians, they were the same war interrupted by two decades, and similar in that combatants killed more efficiently than armies throughout history ever had, the differences between the wars were significant. In terms of the physical impact of the fighting, the impact on

civilians, the action on the battlefield at mid-war, and the aftermaths, World Wars I and II differed in ways that matter to us decades later. Recently, the wars in Iraq, Afghanistan, and Bosnia have involved an alliance of nations pitted against single nations; but we have not seen, since the two world wars, grand alliances moving vast armies across continents. The destruction implied by such action is almost unthinkable today. Warfare is changing, and "stateless" combatants like Hamas and Al Qaeda wreak destruction of their own. But we may never see, one hopes, the devastation that follows when multiple nations on opposing sides of a conflict throw millions of soldiers--and civilians--into harm's way.

## The Strategy of the Exam Response

The general strategy of this argument is an organization by *criteria*. The writer argues that although the two world wars exhibited some similarities, the differences between the two conflicts were more significant. Note that the writer's thesis doesn't merely establish these significant differences; it enumerates them in a way that anticipates both the content and the structure of the response to follow.

In argument terms, the *claim* the writer makes is the conclusion that the two global conflicts were significantly different, if superficially similar. The *assumption* is that careful attention to the impact of the wars upon cities and civilian populations and to the consequences of the Allied victories is the key to understanding the differences between them. The *support* comes in the form of historical facts regarding the level of casualties, the scope of destruction, the theaters of conflict, the events following the conclusions of the wars, and so on.

- **Paragraph 1:** The writer begins by commenting on the unprecedented level of destruction of World Wars I and II and concludes with the thesis summarizing the key similarities and differences.

- **Paragraph 2:** The writer summarizes the key similarities in the two wars: the wars' causes, their combatants, their global scope, the level of destructiveness made possible by modern weaponry.

- **Paragraph 3:** The writer discusses the first of the key differences: the fact that the battlegrounds of World War I were largely rural, but in World War II cities were targeted and destroyed.

- **Paragraph 4:** The writer discusses the second of the key differences: the impact on civilians. In World War I, civilians were generally spared from the direct effects of combat; in World War II, civilians were targeted by the Nazis for systematic displacement and destruction.

- **Paragraph 5:** The writer discusses the third key difference: Combat operations during the middle phase of World War I were characterized by static trench warfare. During World War II, in contrast, there were no major combat operations in Nazi-occupied Western Europe during the middle phase of the conflict.

- **Paragraph 6:** The writer focuses on the fourth key difference: the aftermath of the two wars. After World War I, the victors imposed harsh conditions on defeated Germany, leading to the rise of Hitler and the Second World War. After World War II, the Allies helped Germany rebuild and thrive. However, the Soviet victory in 1945 led to its postwar domination of Eastern Europe.

- **Paragraph 7:** In the conclusion, the writer sums up the key similarities and differences just covered and makes additional comments about the course of more recent wars since World War II. In this way, the writer responds to the questions posed at the end of the assignment: "What have you learned? What can your comparative analysis teach us?"

## Avoid Common Fallacies in Developing and Using Support

In Chapter 2, in the section on critical reading, we considered criteria that, as a reader, you may use for evaluating informative and persuasive writing (see pp. 40–41, 44–53). We discussed how you can assess the accuracy, the significance, and the author's interpretation of the information presented. We also considered the importance in good argument of clearly defined key terms and the pitfalls of emotionally loaded language. Finally, we saw how to recognize such logical fallacies as either/or reasoning, faulty cause-and-effect reasoning, hasty generalization, and false analogy. As a writer, no less than as a critical reader, you need to be aware of these common problems and to avoid them.

Be aware, also, of your responsibility to cite source materials appropriately. When you quote a source, double- and triple-check that you have done so accurately. When you summarize or paraphrase, take care to use your own language and sentence structures (though you can, of course, also quote within these forms). When you refer to someone else's idea—even if you are not quoting, summarizing, or paraphrasing—give the source credit. By being ethical about the use of sources, you uphold the highest standards of the academic community.

## THE EXPLANATORY SYNTHESIS

Some of the papers you write in college will be more or less explanatory (as opposed to argumentative) in nature. An explanation helps readers understand a topic. Writers explain when they divide a subject into its component parts and present them to the reader in a clear and orderly fashion. Explanations may entail descriptions that re-create in words some object, place, emotion, event, sequence of events, or state of affairs. As a student reporter, you may need to explain an event—to relate when, where, and how it took place. In a science lab, you would observe the conditions and results of an experiment and record them for review by others. In a political science course, you might review research on a particular subject—say, the complexities underlying the debate over gay marriage—and then present the results of your research to your professor and the members of your class.

Your job in writing an explanatory synthesis—or in writing the explanatory portion of an argument synthesis—is not to argue a particular point, but rather *to present the facts in a reasonably objective manner.* Explanatory papers, like other academic papers, should be based on a thesis. But the purpose of a thesis in an explanatory paper is less to advance a particular opinion than it is to focus the various facts contained in the paper.

The explanatory synthesis is fairly modest in purpose. It emphasizes the materials in the sources, not the writer's interpretation of them. Because your reader is not always in a position to read your sources, this kind of synthesis, if done well, can be very informative. But the main characteristic of the explanatory synthesis is that it is designed more to *inform* than to *persuade.* As the writer of an explanatory synthesis, you remain for the most part a detached observer.

## Model Explanatory Synthesis

Let's demonstrate the difference between an argument synthesis and an explanatory synthesis on the same subject. This is the same kind of demonstration we offered early in this chapter (pp. 77–79) in the contrast between a news article and an editorial on the same topic: the sentencing of those involved in the Abu Ghraib scandal: One source is primarily explanatory; the other is strongly argumentative. Below is a new, highly excerpted version of the argument synthesis on balancing privacy rights and safety (pp. 105–115) with the argument components removed and the explanatory components reinforced. The writer is now, in effect, simply reporting on the debate rather than commenting upon it or offering his opinions and recommendations. He is now writing an explanatory synthesis.

Much of the content (including the parts represented by ellipses) remains the same as in the argument synthesis— which illustrates the fact that explanation often plays a pivotal role in making arguments. We highlight the sentences and attributive phrases (such as "officials hope"), as well as the revamped the thesis, that help convert this paper from an argument synthesis to an explanatory synthesis.

### EXPLANTORY SYNTHESIS

(Thesis and topic sentences are highlighted.)

---

Privacy vs. Safety in the Wake of Virginia Tech

1    On April 16, 2007, Seung Hui Cho, a mentally ill Student at Virginia Polytechnic Institute, shot to death 32 fellow students and faculty members, and injured 17 others, before killing himself. It was the worst mass shooting in U.S. history, and the fact that it took place on a college campus lent a special horror to the event. . . .

3    The shootings at Virginia Tech demonstrate, in the most horrifying way, the need for secure college campuses. Nevertheless, privacy remains a crucial right to most Americans—including college students, many of whom for the first time are exercising their prerogatives as adults.

Many students who pose no threat to anyone will object strenuously to university administrators peering into and making judgments about their private lives. Some might be unwilling to seek professional therapy if they knew that the records of their counseling sessions might be released to their parents or to other students. As they struggled to understand what had gone wrong at Virginia Tech, college officials, mental health professionals, lawmakers, and others attempted to develop new policies and procedures that would help prevent another such incident and also balance the demands of student privacy and campus safety.

4    In these days of Facebook and reality TV, the notion of privacy rights, particularly for young people, may seem quaint. . . .

13    One can easily understand how parents would be outraged by the MIT position. No parent would willingly let his or her child enter an environment where that child's safety cannot be assured. Just as the first priority for any government is to protect its citizens, the  first priority of an educational institution must be to keep its students safe. But how, exactly, to keep students safe, college officials concede, is a complicated matter.

14    One of the " key findings" of the Virginia Tech Review Panel was that federal privacy laws, properly interpreted and implemented, do nothing to endanger campus safety. "In reality," the panel concluded, "federal lawsand their state counterparts afford ample leeway to share information in potentially dangerous situations (Virginia Tech Review 2). So the problem at Virginia Tech, according to the

18

panel, was not the federal government's policy; it was the university's own practices based on a faculty interpretation of that policy. The breakdown began with the failure of Virgina Tech officials to understand federal privacy laws. . . .

This open communication between university officials presumably will also help with delicate judgments—whether, for example, a student's violent story written for a creative writing class is an indication of mental instability or simply an early work by the next Stephen King ("Virginia Tech Massacre" 1).

19–20

The tragic events at Virginia Tech have spurred renewed debate over the often competing claims of student privacy and campus safety. During the course of this debate universities have undertaken important modifications in their procedures. These new policies involve a more proactive approach to student mental health and improvements in communication between departments, such as those at the University of Kentucky. Such measures, officials hope, will not only bring confidential help to the troubled students who need it, they will also improve the safety of the larger college community. At the same time, they expect that these measures will preserve hard-won privacy rights on campus.

## The Strategy of the Explanatory Synthesis

In developing this explanatory synthesis, the writer uses much of the same wording—that is, the same facts and claims—that appears in the argument synthesis. But the writer keeps his own opinions to himself. Note especially the new thesis: the original argument thesis that takes a strong position ("we should resist rolling back federal rules") has been replaced by an explanatory thesis reflecting a more neutral stance ("college officials . . . and others attempted to develop new policies and procedures"). Note also such attributive phrases as "they expect that," which serve to relocate strongly held views away from the writer and credit them to others. As for the conclusion, note that the emphasis remains on explaining, not on finding fault or giving credit.

## SUMMARY

In this chapter we've considered two main types of synthesis: the *argument synthesis* and the *explanatory synthesis*. Although for ease of comprehension we've placed them in separate categories, the types are not mutually exclusive. Both argument syntheses and explanatory syntheses often involve elements of one another. Which format you choose will depend upon your *purpose* and the method that you decide is best suited to achieve that purpose.

If your main purpose is to help your audience understand a particular subject, and in particular to help them understand the essential elements or significance of that subject, then you will be composing an explanatory synthesis. If your main purpose, on the other hand, is to persuade your audience to agree with your viewpoint on a subject, or to change their minds, or to decide upon a particular course of action, then you will be composing an argument synthesis. If one effective technique for making your case is to establish similarities or differences between your subject and another one, then you will compose a comparison-and-contrast synthesis—which may well be only *part* of a larger synthesis.

In planning and drafting these syntheses, you can draw upon a variety of strategies: supporting your claims by summarizing, paraphrasing, and quoting from your sources; and choosing from among formats such as climactic or conventional order, counterargument, and concession to help you achieve your purpose.

The strategies of synthesis you've practiced in this chapter will be important in composing a research paper, the successful execution of which involves all of the skills of summary, critique, and synthesis that we've discussed so far.

# 4

# Analysis

## WHAT IS AN ANALYSIS?

An *analysis* is an argument in which you study the parts of something to understand how it works, what it means, or why it might be significant. The writer of an analysis uses an analytical tool: a *principle* or *definition* on the basis of which an object, an event, or a behavior can be divided into parts and examined. Here are excerpts from two analyses of L. Frank Baum's *The Wizard of Oz:*

> At the dawn of adolescence, the very time she should start to distance herself from Aunt Em and Uncle Henry, the surrogate parents who raised her on their Kansas farm, Dorothy Gale experiences a hurtful reawakening of her fear that these loved ones will be rudely ripped from her, especially her Aunt (Em—M for Mother!). [Harvey Greenberg, *The Movies on Your* Mind (New York: Dutton, 1975).]

> [*The Wizard of Oz*] was originally written as a political allegory about grass-roots protest. It may seem harder to believe than Emerald City, but the Tin Woodsman is the industrial worker, the Scarecrow [is] the struggling farmer, and the Wizard is the president, who is powerful only as long as he succeeds in deceiving the people. [Peter Dreier, "Oz Was Almost Reality," *Cleveland Plain Dealer* September 3, 1989.]

As these paragraphs suggest, what you discover through an analysis depends entirely on the principle or definition you use to make your insights. Is *The Wizard of Oz* the story of a girl's psychological development, or is it a story about politics? The answer is *both.* In the first example, the psychiatrist Harvey Greenberg applies the principles of his profession

**145**

and, not surprisingly, sees *The Wizard of Oz* in psychological terms. In the second example, a newspaper reporter applies the political theories of Karl Marx and, again not surprisingly, discovers a story about politics.

Different as they are, these analyses share an important quality: Each is the result of a specific principle or definition used as a tool to divide an object into parts in order to see what it means and how it works. The writer's choice of analytical tool simultaneously creates and limits the possibilities for analysis. Thus, working with the principles of Freud, Harvey Greenberg sees *The Wizard of Oz* in psychological, not political, terms; working with the theories of Karl Marx, Peter Dreier understands the movie in terms of the economic relationships among characters. It's as if the writer of an analysis who adopts one analytical tool puts on a pair of glasses and sees an object in a specific way. Another writer, using a different tool (and a different pair of glasses), sees the object differently.

You might protest: Are there as many analyses of *The Wizard of Oz* as there are people to read it? Yes, or at least as many analyses as there are analytical tools. This does not mean that all analyses are equally valid or useful. Each writer must convince the reader. In creating an essay of analysis, the writer must

---

### WHERE DO WE FIND WRITTEN ANALYSES?

*Here are just a few types of writing that involve analysis*

#### Academic Writing

- **Experimental and lab reports**  analyze the meaning or implications of the study results in the Discussion section.
- **Research papers**  analyze information in sources or apply theories to material being reported.

- **Process analysis** breaks down the steps or stages involved in completing a process.
- **Literary analysis** analyzes characterization, plot, imagery, or other elements in works of literature.
- **Essay exams** demonstrate understanding of course material by analyzing data using course concepts.

### Workplace Writing

- **Grant proposals** analyze the issues you seek funding for in order to address them.
- **Reviews of the arts** employ dramatic or literary analysis to assess artistic works.
- **Business plans** break down and analyze capital outlays, expenditures, profits, materials, and the like.
- **Medical charts** record analytical thinking and writing in relation to patient symptoms and possible options.
- **Legal briefs** break down and analyze facts of cases and elements of legal precedents and apply legal rulings and precedents to new situations.
- **Case studies** describe and analyze the particulars of a specific medical, social service, advertising, or business case.

organize a series of related insights, using the analytical tool to examine first one part and then another of the object being studied. To read Harvey Greenberg's essay on *The Wizard of Oz* is to find paragraph after paragraph of related insights—first about Aunt Em, then the Wicked Witch, then Toto, and then the Wizard. All these insights point to Greenberg's single conclusion: that "Dorothy's 'trip' is a marvelous metaphor for the psychological journey every adolescent must make." Without Greenberg's analysis, we would probably not have thought about the movie as a psychological journey. This is precisely the power of an analysis: its ability to reveal objects or events in ways we would not otherwise have considered.

The writer's challenge is to convince readers that (1) the analytical tool being applied is legitimate and well matched to the object being studied; and (2) the analytical tool is being used systematically to divide the object into parts and to make a coherent, meaningful statement about these parts and the object as a whole.

## DEMONSTRATION: ANALYSIS

Two examples of analyses follow. The first was written by a professional writer. The second was written by a student in response to an assignment in his sociology class. Each analysis illustrates the two defining features of analysis just discussed: a statement of an analytical principle or definition, and the use of that principle or definition in closely examining an object, behavior, or event. As you read, try to identify these features. An exercise with questions for discussion follows each example.

### The Plug-In Drug

#### Marie Winn

*The following analysis of television viewing as an addictive behavior appeared originally in Marie Winn's book,* The Plug-In Drug: Television, Computers, and Family Life, 2002. *A writer and media critic, Winn has been interested in the effects of television on both individuals and the larger culture. In this passage, she carefully defines the term addiction and then applies it systematically to the behavior under study.*

1 The word "addiction" is often used loosely and wryly in conversation. People will refer to themselves as "mystery-book addicts" or "cookie addicts." E. B. White wrote of his annual surge of interest in gardening: "We are hooked and are making an attempt to kick

the habit." Yet nobody really believes that reading mysteries or ordering seeds by catalogue is serious enough to be compared with addictions to heroin or alcohol. In these cases the word "addiction" is used jokingly to denote a tendency to overindulge in some pleasurable activity.

2    People often refer to being "hooked on TV." Does this, too, fall into the lighthearted category of cookie eating and other pleasures that people pursue with unusual intensity? Or is there a kind of television viewing that falls into the more serious category of destructive addiction?

3    Not unlike drugs or alcohol, the television experience allows the participant to blot out the real world and enter into a pleasurable and passive mental state. To be sure, other experiences, notably reading, also provide a temporary respite from reality. But it's much easier to stop reading and return to reality than to stop watching television. The entry into another world offered by reading includes an easily accessible return ticket. The entry via television does not. In this way television viewing, for those vulnerable to addiction, is more like drinking or taking drugs—once you start it's hard to stop.

4    Just as alcoholics are only vaguely aware of their addiction, feeling that they control their drinking more than they really do ("I can cut it out any time I want—I just like to have three or four drinks before dinner"), many people overestimate their control over television watching. Even as they put off other activities to spend hour after hour watching television, they feel they could easily resume living in a different, less passive style. But somehow or other while the television set is present in their homes, it just stays on. With television's easy gratifications available, those other activities seem to take too much effort.

5    A heavy viewer (a college English instructor) observes:

> I find television almost irresistible. When the set is on, I cannot ignore it. I can't turn it off. I feel sapped, will-less, enervated. As I reach out to turn off the set, the strength goes out of my arms. So I sit there for hours and hours.

6      Self-confessed television addicts often feel they "ought" to do other things—but the fact that they don't read and don't plant their garden or sew or crochet or play games or have conversations means that those activities are no longer as desirable as television viewing. In a way, the lives of heavy viewers are as unbalanced by their television "habit" as drug addicts' or alcoholics' lives. They are living in a holding pattern, as it were, passing up the activities that lead to growth or development or a sense of accomplishment. This is one reason people talk about their television viewing so ruefully, so apologetically. They are aware that it is an unproductive experience, that by any human measure almost any other endeavor is more worthwhile.

7      It is the adverse effect of television viewing on the lives of so many people that makes it feel like a serious addiction. The television habit distorts the sense of time. It renders other experiences vague and curiously unreal while taking on a greater reality for itself. It weakens relationships by reducing and sometimes eliminating normal opportunities for talking, for communicating.

8      And yet television does not satisfy, else why would the viewer continue to watch hour after hour, day after day? "The measure of health," wrote the psychiatrist Lawrence Kubie, "is flexibility . . . and especially the freedom to cease when sated." But heavy television viewers can never be sated with their television experiences. These do not provide the true nourishment that satiation requires, and thus they find that they cannot stop watching.

---

Edward Peselman wrote the following paper as a first-semester sophomore, in response to this assignment from his sociology professor:

Read Chapter 3, "The Paradoxes of Power," in Randall Collins's *Sociological Insight: An Introduction to Non-Obvious*

*Sociology* (2nd ed., 1992). Use any of Collins's observations to examine the sociology of power in a group with which you are familiar. Write for readers much like yourself: freshmen or sophomores who have taken one course in sociology. Your object in this paper is to use Collins as a way of learning something "nonobvious" about a group to which you belong or have belonged.

Note: The citations are in APA style. (See pp. 178–179.)

## MODEL ANALYSIS

Coming Apart    1

Edward Peselman
Sociology of Everyday Life
Murray State University
23 March 2008

The Coming Apart of a Dorm Society

1    During my first year of college, I lived in a dormitory, like most freshmen on campus. We inhabitants of the dorm came from different cultural and economic backgrounds. Not surprisingly, we brought with us many of the traits found in people outside of college. Like many on the outside, we in the dorm sought personal power at the expense of others. The gaining and maintaining of power can be an ugly business, and I saw people hurt and in turn hurt others all for the sake of securing a place in the dorm's prized social order. Not until one of us challenged that order did I realize how fragile it was.

2    Randall Collins, a sociologist at the University of California, Riverside, defines the exercise of power as the attempt "to make something happen in society" (1992, p. 61). A society can be understood as something as large and complex as "American society"; something more sharply defined, such as a corporate or organizational society; or something smaller still—a dorm society like my own, consisting of six 18-year-old men who lived at one end of a dormitory floor in an all-male dorm.

3    In my freshman year, my society was a tiny but distinctive social group in which people exercised power. I lived with two roommates, Dozer and Reggie. Dozer was an emotionally unstable, excitable individual who vented his energy through anger. His insecurity and moodiness contributed to his difficulty in making friends. Reggie was a friendly, happy-go-lucky sort who seldom displayed emotions other than contentedness. He was shy when encountering new people, but when placed in a socially comfortable situation he would talk for hours.

4    Eric and Marc lived across the hall from us and therefore spent a considerable amount of time in our room. Eric could be cynical and was often blunt: He seldom hesitated when sharing his frank and sometimes unflattering opinions. He commanded a grudging respect in the dorm. Marc could be very moody and, sometimes, was violent. His temper and stubborn streak made him particularly susceptible to conflict. The final member of our miniature society was Benjamin, cheerful yet insecure. Benjamin had certain

characteristics which many considered effeminate, and he
was often teased about his sexuality—which in turn made
him insecure. He was naturally friendly but, because of the
abuse he took, he largely kept to himself. He would join us
occasionally for a pizza or late-night television.

5    Together, we formed an independent social structure.
Going out to parties together, playing cards, watching
television, playing ball: These were the activities through
which we got to know each other and through which we
established the basic pecking order of our community. Much
like a colony of baboons, we established a hierarchy based
on power relationships. According to Collins, what a powerful person wishes to happen must be achieved by controlling
others. Collins's observation can help to define who had
how much power in our social group. In the dorm, Marc and
Eric clearly had the most power. Everyone feared them and
agreed to do pretty much what they wanted. Through violent
words or threats of violence, they got their way. I was next in
line: I wouldn't dare to manipulate Marc or Eric, but the
others I could manage through occasional quips. Reggie,
then Dozer, and finally Benjamin.

6    Up and down the pecking order, we exercised control
through macho taunts and challenges. Collins writes that
"individuals who manage to be powerful and get their own
way must do so by going along with the laws of social
organization, not by contradicting them" (p. 61). Until mid-
year, our dorm motto could have read: "You win through
rudeness and intimidation." Eric gained power with his
frequent and brutal assessments of everyone's behavior.
Marc gained power with his temper—which, when lost,

made everyone run for cover. Those who were not rude and
intimidating drifted to the bottom of our social world.
Reggie was quiet and unemotional, which allowed us to
take advantage of him because we knew he would back
down if pressed in an argument. Yet Reggie understood that
on a "power scale" he stood above Dozer and often shared
in the group's tactics to get Dozer's food (his parents were
forever sending him care packages). Dozer, in turn, seldom
missed opportunities to take swipes at Benjamin, with references to his sexuality. From the very first week of school,
Benjamin could never—and never wanted to—compete
against Eric's bluntness or Marc's temper. Still, Benjamin
hung out with us. He lived in our corner of the dorm, and
he wanted to be friendly. But everyone, including
Benjamin, understood that he occupied the lowest spot in
the order.

7          That is, until he left mid-year. According to Collins, "any
social arrangement works because people avoid questioning
it most of the time" (p. 74). The inverse of this principle is as
follows: When a social arrangement is questioned, that
arrangement can fall apart. The more fragile the arrangement
(the flimsier the values on which it is based), the more quickly it will crumble. For the entire first semester, no one questioned our rude, macho rules, and because of them we
pigeon-holed Benjamin as a wimp. In our dorm society,
gentle men had no power. To say the least, ours was not a
compassionate community. From a distance of one year, I am
shocked to have been a member of it. Nonetheless, we had
created a mini-society that somehow served our needs.

8    At the beginning of the second semester, we
found Benjamin packing up his room. Marc, who was
walking down the hall, stopped by and said something like:
"Hey buddy, the kitchen get too hot for you?" I was there,
and I saw Benjamin turn around and say: "Do you practice
at being such a _____, or does it come naturally? I've
never met anybody who felt so good about making other
people feel lousy. You'd better get yourself a job in the army
or in the prison system, because no one else is going to put
up with your _____." Marc said something in a raised
voice. I stepped between them, and Benjamin said: "Get
out." I was cheering.

9    Benjamin moved into an off-campus apartment with his
girlfriend. This astonished us, first because of his effeminate manner (we didn't know he had a girlfriend) and
second because none of the rest of us had been seeing girls
much (though we talked about it constantly). Here was
Benjamin, the gentlest among us, and he blew a hole in our
macho society. Our social order never really recovered,
which suggests its flimsy values. People in the dorm mostly
went their own ways during the second semester. I'm not
surprised, and I was more than a little grateful. Like most
people in the dorm, save for Eric and Marc, I both got my
lumps and I gave them, and I never felt good about either.
Like Benjamin, I wanted to fit in with my new social sur-
roundings. Unlike him, I didn't have the courage to challenge the unfairness of what I saw.

10    By chance, six of us were thrown together into a dorm
and were expected, on the basis of proximity alone, to

develop a friendship. What we did was sink to the lowest possible denominator. Lacking any real basis for friendship, we allowed the forceful, macho personalities of Marc and Eric to set the rules, which for one semester we all subscribed to—even those who suffered.

11          The macho rudeness couldn't last, and I'm glad it was Benjamin who brought us down. By leaving, he showed a different and a superior kind of power. I doubt he was reading Randall Collins at the time, but he somehow had come to Collins's same insight: As long as he played by the rules of our group, he suffered because those rules placed him far down in the dorm's pecking order. Even by participating in pleasant activities, like going out for pizza, Benjamin supported a social system that ridiculed him. Some systems are so oppressive and small-minded that they can't be changed from the inside. They've got to be torn down. Benjamin had to move, and in moving he made me (at least) question the basis of my dorm friendships.

[new page]

### Reference

Collins, R. (1992). *Sociological insight: An introduction to non-obvious sociology* (2nd ed.). New York: Oxford University Press.

# HOW TO WRITE ANALYSES

## Consider Your Purpose

Whether you are assigned a topic to write on or are left to your own devices, you inevitably face this question: What is my idea? Like every paper, an analysis has at its heart an idea you want to convey. For Edward Peselman, it was the idea that a social order based on flimsy values is not strong enough to sustain a direct challenge to its power and thus will fall apart eventually. From beginning to end, Peselman advances this one idea: first, by introducing readers to the dorm society he will analyze; next, by introducing principles of analysis (from Randall Collins); and finally, by examining his dorm relationships in light of those principles. The entire set of analytical insights coheres as a paper because the insights are *related* and point to Peselman's single idea.

Peselman's paper offers a good example of the personal uses to which analysis can be put. Notice that he gravitates toward events in his life that confuse him and about which he wants some clarity. Such topics can be especially fruitful for analysis because you know the particulars well and can provide readers with details; you view the topic with some puzzlement; and, through the application of your analytical tool, you may come to understand it. When you select topics to analyze from your experience, you provide yourself with a motivation to write and learn. When you are motivated in this way, you spark the interest of readers.

Using Randall Collins as a guide, Edward Peselman returns again and again to the events of his freshman year in the dormitory. We sense that Peselman himself wants to understand what happened in that dorm. He writes, "I saw people hurt and in turn hurt others all for the sake of securing a place in the dorm's prized social order." Peselman does not approve of what happened, and the analysis he launches is meant to help him understand.

## Locate an Analytical Principle

When you are given an assignment that asks for analysis, use two specific reading strategies to identify principles and definitions in source materials.

- **Look for a sentence that makes a general statement about the way something works.** The statement may strike you as a rule or a law. The line that Edward Peselman quotes from Randall Collins has this quality: "[A]ny social arrangement works because people avoid questioning it most of the time." Such statements are generalizations—conclusions to sometimes complicated and extensive arguments. You can use these conclusions to guide your own analyses as long as you are aware that for some audiences you will need to re-create and defend the arguments that resulted in these conclusions.

- **Look for statements that take this form: X can be defined as (or X consists of) A, B, and C.** The specific elements of the definition—A, B, and C—are what you use to identify and analyze parts of the object being studied. You've seen an example of this approach in Marie Winn's multipart definition of addiction, which she uses to analyze television viewing. As a reader looking for definitions suitable for conducting an analysis, you might come across Winn's definition of addiction and then use it for your own purposes, perhaps to analyze the playing of video games as an addiction.

Essential to any analysis is the validity of the principle or definition being applied, the analytical tool. Make yourself aware, as both writer and reader, of a tool's strengths and limitations. Pose these questions of the analytical principles and definitions you use: Are they accurate? Are they well accepted? Do *you* accept them? What are the arguments against them? What are their limitations? Since every principle or definition used in an analysis is the end product of an argument, you are entitled—even obligated—to challenge it. If the analytical tool is flawed, the analysis that follows from it will be flawed.

A page from Collins's *Sociological Insight* follows; Edward Peselman uses a key sentence from this extract as an analytical tool in his essay on power relations in his dorm (see p. 154). Notice that Peselman underlines the sentence he will use in his analysis.

1 Try this experiment some time. When you are talking to someone, make them explain everything they say that isn't completely clear. The result, you will discover, is a series of uninterrupted interruptions:

A: Hi, how are you doing?
B: What do you mean when you say "how"?
A: You know. What's happening with you?
B: What do you mean, "happening"?
A: Happening, you know, what's going on.
B: I'm sorry. Could you explain what you mean
  by "what"?
A: What do you mean, what do I mean? Do you want to
  talk to me or not?

2     It is obvious that this sort of questioning could go on endlessly, at any rate if the listener doesn't get very angry and punch you in the mouth. But it illustrates two important points. First, virtually everything can be called into question. We are able to get along with other people not because everything is clearly spelled out, but because we are willing to take most things people say without explanation. Harold Garfinkel, who actually performed this sort of experiment, points out that there is an infinite regress of assumptions that go into any act of social communication. Moreover, some expressions are simply not explainable in words at all. A word like "you," or "here," or "now" is what Garfinkel calls "indexical." You have to know what it means already; it can't be explained.

3     "What do you mean by 'you'?"

4    "I mean *you, you!*" About all that can be done here is point your finger.

5    The second point is that people get mad when they are pressed to explain things that they ordinarily take for granted. This is because they very quickly see that explanations could go on forever and the questions will never be answered. If you really demanded a full explanation of everything you hear, you could stop the conversation from ever getting past its first sentence. The real significance of this for a sociological understanding of the way the world is put together is not the anger, however. It is the fact that people try to avoid these sorts of situations. They tacitly recognize that we have to avoid these endless lines of questioning. Sometimes small children will start asking an endless series of "whys," but adults discourage this.

6    In sum, <u>any social arrangement works because people avoid questioning it most of the time</u>. That does not mean that people do not get into arguments or disputes about just what ought to be done from time to time. But to have a dispute already implies there is a considerable area of agreement. An office manager may dispute with a clerk over just how to take care of some business letter, but they at any rate know more or less what they are disputing about. They do not get off into a . . . series of questions over just what is meant by everything that is said. You could very quickly dissolve the organization into nothingness if you followed that route: there would be no communication at all, even about what the disagreement is over.

7    Social organization is possible because people maintain a certain level of focus. If they focus on one thing, even if only to disagree about it, they are taking many other things for granted, thereby reinforcing their social reality.

The statement that Peselman has underlined—"any social arrangement works because people avoid questioning it most of the time"—is the end result of an argument that takes Collins several paragraphs to develop. Peselman agrees with the conclusion and uses it in paragraph 7 of his analysis. Observe that for his own purposes Peselman does *not* reconstruct Collins's argument. He selects *only* Collins's conclusion and then imports that into his analysis, which concerns an entirely different subject. Once he identifies in Collins a principle he can use in his analysis, he converts the principle into questions that he then directs to his topic, life in his freshman dorm. Two questions follow directly from Collins's insight:

1. What was the social arrangement in the dorm?
2. How was this social arrangement questioned?

Peselman clearly defines his dormitory's social arrangement in paragraphs 3–6 (with the help of another principle borrowed from Collins). Beginning with paragraph 7, he explores how one member of his dorm questioned that arrangement:

> That is, until he left mid-year. According to Collins, "any social arrangement works because people avoid questioning it most of the time" (p. 74). The inverse of this principle is as follows: When a social arrangement is questioned, that arrangement can fall apart. The more fragile the arrangement (the flimsier the values on which it is based), the more quickly it will crumble. For the entire first semester, no one questioned our rude, macho rules, and because of them we pigeon-holed Benjamin as a wimp. In our dorm society, gentle men had no power. To say the least, ours was not a compassionate community. From a distance of one year, I am shocked to have been a member of it. Nonetheless, we had created a mini-society that somehow served our needs.

## Formulate a Thesis

An analysis is a two-part argument. The first part states and establishes the writer's agreement with a certain principle or definition.

### Part One of the Argument

This first part of the argument essentially takes this form:

**Claim #1:** Principle X (or definition X) is valuable.

Principle X can be a theory as encompassing and abstract as the statement that *myths are the enemy of truth.* Principle X can be as modest as the definition of a term such as *addiction* or *comfort.* As you move from one subject area to another, the principles and definitions you use for analysis will change, as these assignments illustrate:

> **Sociology:** *Write a paper in which you place yourself in American society by locating both your absolute position and relative rank on each single criterion of social stratification used by Lenski & Lenski. For each criterion, state whether you have attained your social position by yourself or if you have "inherited" that status from your parents.*

> **Literature:** *Apply principles of Jungian psychology to Hawthorne's "Young Goodman Brown." In your reading of the story, apply Jung's principles of the* shadow, persona, *and* anima.

> **Physics:** *Use Newton's second law* ($F = ma$) *to analyze the acceleration of a fixed pulley, from which two weights hang:* $m_1$ *(.45 kg) and* $m_2$ *(.90 kg). Explain in a paragraph the principle of Newton's law and your method of applying it to solve the problem. Assume your reader is not comfortable with mathematical explanations: do not use equations in your paragraph.*

> **Finance:** *Using Guidford C. Babcock's "Concept of Sustainable Growth" [Financial Analysis 26 (May–June 1970): 108–14], analyze the stock price appreciation of the XYZ Corporation, figures for which are attached.*

The analytical tools to be applied in these assignments must be appropriate to the discipline. Writing in response to the sociology assignment, you would use sociological principles developed by Lenski and Lenski. In your literature class, you would use principles of Jungian psychology; in physics, Newton's second law; and in finance, a particular writer's concept of "sustainable growth." But whatever discipline you are working in, the first part of your analysis will clearly state which (and whose) principles and definitions you are applying. For audiences unfamiliar with these principles, you will need to explain them; if you anticipate objections, you will need to argue that they are legitimate principles capable of helping you conduct the analysis.

## GUIDELINES FOR WRITING ANALYSIS

Unless you are asked to follow a specialized format, especially in the sciences or the social sciences, you can present your analysis as a paper by following the guidelines below. As you move from one class to another, from discipline to discipline, the principles and definitions you use as the basis for your analyses will change, but the following basic components of analysis will remain the same.

- *Create a context for your analysis.* Introduce and summarize for readers the object, event, or behavior to be analyzed. Present a strong case about why an analysis is needed: Give yourself a motivation to write, and give readers a motivation to read. Consider setting out a problem, puzzle, or question to be investigated.
- *Introduce and summarize the key definition or principle that will form the basis of your analysis.* Plan to devote an early part of your analysis to arguing for the validity of this principle or definition if your audience is not likely to understand it or if they are likely to think that the principle or definition is not valuable.
- *Analyze your topic.* Systematically apply elements of this definition or principle to parts of the activity or object under study. You can do this by posing specific questions, based on your analytic principle or definition, about the object. Discuss what you find part by part (organized perhaps by question), in clearly defined sections of the essay.

*(Continued on next page)*

- *Conclude by stating clearly what is significant about your analysis.* When considering your analytical paper as a whole, what new or interesting insights have you made concerning the object under study? To what extent has your application of the definition or principle helped you to explain how the object works, what it might mean, or why it is significant?

*Part Two of the Argument*

In the second part of an analysis, you *apply* specific parts of your principle or definition to the topic at hand. Regardless of how it is worded, this second argument in an analysis can be rephrased to take this form:

**Claim #2:** By applying principle (or definition) X, we can understand *(topic)* as *(conclusion based on analysis)*.

This is your thesis, the main idea of your analytical paper. Fill in the first blank with the specific object, event, or behavior you are examining. Fill in the second blank with your conclusion about the meaning or significance of this object, based on the insights you made during your analysis. Mary Winn completes the second claim of her analysis this way:

By applying my multipart definition, we can understand *television viewing* as *an addiction*.

## Develop an Organizational Plan

You will benefit enormously in the writing of a first draft if you plan out the logic of your analysis. Turn key elements of your analytical principle or definition into questions and then develop the paragraph-by-paragraph logic of the paper.

### Turning Key Elements of a Principle or a Definition into Questions

Prepare for an analysis by phrasing questions based on the definition or principle you are going to apply, and then by directing those questions to the activity or object to be studied. The method is straightforward: State as clearly as possible the principle or definition to be applied. Divide the principle or definition into its parts and, using each part, form a question. For example, Marie Winn develops a multipart definition of addiction, each part of which is readily turned into a question that she directs at a specific behavior: television viewing. Her analysis of television viewing can be understood as *responses* to each of her analytical questions. Note that in her brief analysis, Winn does not first define addiction and then analyze television viewing. Rather, *as* she defines aspects of addiction, she analyzes television viewing.

### Developing the Paragraph-by-Paragraph Logic of Your Paper

The following paragraph from Edward Peselman's essay illustrates the typical logic of a paragraph in an analytical essay:

> Up and down the pecking order, we exercised control through macho taunts and challenges. Collins writes that "individuals who manage to be powerful and get their own way must do so by going along with the laws of social organization, not by contradicting them" (p. 61). Until mid-year, our dorm motto could have read: "You win through rudeness and intimidation." Eric gained power with his frequent and brutal assessments of everyone's behavior. Marc gained power with his temper—which, when lost, made everyone run for cover. Those who were not rude and intimidating drifted to the bottom of our social world. Reggie was quiet and unemotional, which allowed us to take advantage of him because we knew he would back down if pressed in an argument. Yet Reggie understood that on a "power scale" he stood above Dozer and often shared in the group's tactics to get Dozer's food (his parents were

forever sending him care packages). Dozer, in turn, seldom missed opportunities to take swipes at Benjamin, with references to his sexuality. From the very first week of school, Benjamin could never—and never wanted to—compete against Eric's bluntness or Marc's temper. Still, Benjamin hung out with us. He lived in our corner of the dorm, and he wanted to be friendly. But everyone, including Benjamin, understood that he occupied the lowest spot in the order.

We see in this paragraph the typical logic of analysis:

- *The writer introduces a specific analytical tool.* Peselman quotes a line from Randall Collins:

    "[I]ndividuals who manage to be powerful and get their own way must do so by going along with the laws of social organization, not by contradicting them."

- *The writer applies this analytical tool to the object being examined.* Peselman states his dorm's law of social organization:

    Until mid-year, our dorm motto could have read: "You win through rudeness and intimidation."

- *The writer uses the tool to identify and then examine the meaning of parts of the object.* Peselman shows how each member (the "parts") of his dorm society conforms to the laws of "social organization":

    Eric gained power with his frequent and brutal assessments of everyone's behavior. Marc gained power with his temper— which, when lost, made everyone run for cover. Those who were not rude and intimidating drifted to the bottom of our social world.

An analytical paper takes shape when a writer creates a series of such paragraphs and then links them with an overall logic. Here is the logical organization of Edward Peselman's paper:

- Paragraph 1: Introduction states a problem—provides a motivation to write and to read.

- Paragraph 2: Randall Collins is introduced—the author whose work will provide principles for analysis.

- Paragraphs 3–4: Background information is provided—the cast of characters in the dorm.

- Paragraphs 5–9: The analysis proceeds—specific parts of dorm life are identified and found significant, using principles from Collins.

- Paragraphs 10–11: Summary and conclusion are provided—the freshman dorm society disintegrates for reasons set out in the analysis. A larger point is made: Some oppressive systems must be torn down.

## Draft and Revise Your Analysis

You will usually need at least two drafts to produce a paper that presents your idea clearly. The biggest changes in your paper will typically come between your first and second drafts. No paper that you write, including an analysis, will be complete until you revise and refine your single compelling idea: your analytical conclusion about what the object, event, or behavior being examined means or how it is significant. You revise and refine by evaluating your first draft, bringing to it many of the same questions you pose when evaluating any piece of writing, including these:

- Are the facts accurate?
- Are my opinions supported by evidence?
- Are the opinions of others authoritative?
- Are my assumptions clearly stated?
- Are key terms clearly defined?
- Is the presentation logical?
- Are all parts of the presentation well developed?
- Are significant opposing points of view presented?

Address these same questions to the first draft of your analysis, and you will have solid information to guide your revision.

### Write an Analysis, Not a Summary

The most common error made in writing analyses—an error that is *fatal* to the form—is to present readers with a summary only. For analyses to succeed, you must *apply* a principle or definition and reach a conclusion about the object, event, or behavior you are examining. By definition, a summary (see Chapter 1) includes none of your own conclusions. Summary is naturally a part of analysis; you will need to summarize the object or activity being examined and, depending on the audience's needs, summarize the principle or definition being applied. But in an analysis you must take the next step and share insights that suggest the meaning or significance of some object, event, or behavior.

### Make Your Analysis Systematic

Analyses should give the reader the sense of a systematic, purposeful examination. Marie Winn's analysis illustrates the point: She sets out specific elements of addictive behavior in separate paragraphs and then uses each, within its paragraph, to analyze television viewing. Winn is systematic in her method, and we are never in doubt about her purpose.

Imagine another analysis in which a writer lays out four elements of a definition and then applies only two, without explaining the logic for omitting the others. Or imagine an analysis in which the writer offers a principle for analysis but directs it to only a half or a third of the object being discussed, without providing a rationale for doing so. In both cases the writer would be failing to deliver on a promise basic to analyses: Once a principle or definition is presented, it should be thoroughly and systematically applied.

### Answer the "So What?" Question

An analysis should make readers *want* to read. It should give readers a sense of getting to the heart of the matter, that what is important in the object or activity under analysis is being laid bare and discussed in revealing ways. If when rereading the first draft of your analysis, you cannot imagine readers saying, "I never thought of _____ this way," then something may be seriously wrong. Reread closely to determine why the paper might leave readers flat and exhausted, as opposed to feeling that they have gained new and important insights. Closely reexamine your own motivations for writing. Have *you* learned anything significant through the analysis? If not, neither will readers, and they will turn away. If you have gained important insights through your analysis, communicate them clearly. At some point, pull together your related insights and say, in effect, "Here's how it all adds up."

### Attribute Sources Appropriately

In an analysis you work with one or two sources and apply insights from them to some object or phenomenon you want to understand more thoroughly. Because you are not synthesizing a great many sources, and because the strength of an analysis derives mostly from *your* application of a principle or definition, the opportunities for not appropriately citing sources are diminished. Take special care to cite and quote, as necessary, the one or two sources you use throughout the analysis.

---

## CRITICAL READING FOR ANALYSIS

- *Read to get a sense of the whole in relation to its parts.* Whether you are clarifying for yourself a principle or a definition to be used in an analysis, or you are reading a text that you will analyze, understand how parts function to create the whole. If a definition or principle consists of parts, use them to organize sections of your analysis. If your goal is to analyze a text, be aware of its structure: Note the title and subtitle; identify the main

*(Continued on next page)*

point and subordinate points and where they are located; break the material into sections.

- *Read to discover relationships within the object being analyzed.* Watch for patterns. When you find them, be alert—for you create an occasion to analyze, to use a principle or definition as a guide in discussing what the pattern may mean.

> In fiction, a pattern might involve responses of characters to events or to each other, the recurrence of certain words or phrasings, images, themes, or turns of plot, (to name a few).
>
> In poetry, a pattern might involve rhyme schemes, rhythm, imagery, figurative or literal language, and more.

The challenge to you as a reader is first to see a pattern (perhaps using a guiding principle or definition to do so) and then to locate other instances of that pattern. Reading carefully in this way prepares you to conduct an analysis.

## ANALYSIS: A TOOL FOR UNDERSTANDING

As this chapter has demonstrated, analysis involves applying principles as a way to probe and understand. With incisive principles guiding your analysis, you will be able to pose questions, observe patterns and relationships, and derive meaning. Do not forget that this meaning will be one of several possible meanings. Someone else, or even you, using different analytical tools, could observe the same phenomena and arrive at very different conclusions regarding meaning or significance. We end the chapter, therefore, as we began it: with the two brief analyses of *The Wizard of Oz*. The conclusions expressed in one look nothing like the conclusions expressed in the other, save for the fact that both seek to interpret the same movie. And yet we can say that both are useful, both reveal meaning.

> At the dawn of adolescence, the very time she should start to distance herself from Aunt Em and Uncle Henry, the surrogate parents who raised her on their Kansas farm, Dorothy Gale experiences a hurtful reawakening of her fear that these loved ones will be rudely ripped from her, especially her Aunt (Em— M for Mother!). [Harvey Greenberg, *The Movies on Your Mind* (New York: Dutton, 1975).]

> [*The Wizard of Oz*] was originally written as a political allegory about grass-roots protest. It may seem harder to believe than Emerald City, but the Tin Woodsman is the industrial worker, the Scarecrow [is] the struggling farmer, and the Wizard is the president, who is powerful only as long as he succeeds in deceiving the people. [Peter Dreier, "Oz Was Almost Reality," *Cleveland Plain Dealer,* September 3, 1989.]

You have seen in this chapter how it is possible for two writers, analyzing the same object or phenomenon but applying different analytical principles, to reach vastly different conclusions about what the object or phenomenon may mean or why it is significant. *The Wizard of Oz* is both an inquiry into the psychology of adolescence and a political allegory. What else the classic film may be awaits revealing with the systematic application of other analytical tools. The insights you gain as a writer of analyses depend entirely on your choice of tools and the subtlety with which you apply them.

# Credits

**CHAPTER 1**

**Page 8:** Reprinted with permission from Alan S. Blinder, "Outsourcing: Bigger Than You Thought," *The American Prospect*, Volume 17, Number 11: October 22, 2006. *The American Prospect*, 2000 L. Street NW, Suite 717, Washington, DC 20036. All rights reserved.

**CHAPTER 2**

**Page 42:** "We Are Not Created Equal in Every Way" by Joan Ryan from *San Francisco Chronicle*, December 12, 2000. Copyright © 2000 by *San Francisco Chronicle*. Reproduced with permission of *San Francisco Chronicle* via Copyright Clearance Center, Inc.

**CHAPTER 3**

**Page 77:** Excerpts from "Private Gets 3 Years for Iraq Prison Abuse" by David S. Cloud, from *The New York Times*, September 28, 2005. Copyright © 2005 by The New York Times. All rights reserved. Used by permission and protected by the Copyright Laws of the United States. The printing, copying, redistribution, or retransmission of the Material without express written permission is prohibited. **Page 78:** Excerpt from "Military Abuse," Globe Editorial, published in *The Boston Globe*, September 28, 2005. Copyright © 2005 Globe Newspaper Company, Inc. Reprinted with permission. Visit The Boston Globe online at www.bostonglobe.com. For more information about reprints, contact PARS International Corp. at 212-221-9595. **Page 88:** "Summary of Key Findings" from "Mass Shootings at Virginia Tech, April 17, 2007: Report of the Review Panel Presented to Governor Kaine, Commonwealth of Virginia, August 2007." Used with permission. **Page 93:** "Virginia Tech Massacre has Altered Campus Mental Health Systems," from The Associated Press, April 14, 2008. Used with permission of The Associated Press, copyright © 2008. All rights reserved.

**CHAPTER 4**

**Page 148:** "Cookies or Heroin?" From The Plug-In Drug, Revised and Updated—25th Anniversary Edition by Marie Winn, copyright © 1977, 1985, 2002 by Marie Winn Miller. Used by permission of Viking Penguin, a division of Penguin Group (USA) Inc. **Page 150:** "The Coming Apart of a Dorm Society" by Edward Peselman. Reprinted by permission of the author.

# Index

Academic writing
 analysis in, 146
 critiques of, 38
 summaries in, 3
 synthesis in, 73
Accuracy of information, 39, 40
Active reading, 37
*Ad hominem* argument, 47–48
*All the King's Men* (Warren), 75
Analogy, false, 51–52
Analysis papers, 3, 73, 147
Analysis writing, 3, 38, 73
 critical reading for, 169–170
 defined, 145–148
 draft and revision of, 167–169
 guidelines for, 163–164
 organizational plan for,
  164–167
 Peselman's demonstration of,
  151–157, 165–167
 principles applied in, 164
 purpose identification for, 157
 reading strategies for, 158–161
 thesis formulation for, 161–163
 as tool, 170–171
 where to find, 146–147
 Winn's demonstration of,
  148–151, 158, 165
Argument writing, 3, 6, 41, 42, 75.
  *See also* Analysis; Persuasive
  writing; Synthesis
 *ad hominem*, 47–48
 climactic order, 124–125
 conventional order for, 125
 counterargument, 104, 126
 elements of, 84–86
 legal, 3, 38, 147
 logical, 46–53, 125
Art review, 147
Associated Press, 93–95
Assumptions, 86
 authors' v. self, 55–57

Author
 assumptions of, 55–57
 disagreement/agreement
  with, 53–57
 primary purpose of, 38–39,
  41–42, 69, 76, 81

"Balancing Privacy and Safety"
  (Harrison), 105–115, 116–121
Baum, L. Frank, 145–147, 171
Begging the question, 52
Book review, 38
*Boston Globe*, 78–79
Bridges. *See* Transitions
Business planning, 3, 38, 74,
  147, 162

Cause and effect, faulty, 48–49
Citation, 36. *See also* Quoted
  material
Climactic order, 124–125
Cloud, David S., 77–78
College-level writing, 4
Collins, Randall, 157–161, 167
Communications assignments
 synthesis in, 74
Comparison-and-contrast
  synthesis, 127, 137
 avoiding fallacies in, 138
 demonstration of, 130–131
 model of, 132–136
 organizational planning,
  128–130
Concession making, 126–127
Counterargument, 104, 126
Crime statistics, 40
Critical reading. *See also* Reading
  process
 analysis writing requiring,
  158–161, 169–170
 critique writing requiring,
  69–70
 evaluation via, 37

Critical reading *(continued)*
  source materials requiring, 72
  summary writing requiring,
    5–6, 37, 38
"A Critique of 'We Are Not
  Created Equal in Every Way'
  by Joan Ryan" (Ralston),
  62–70
Critique writing, 3, 37–38, 53–57
  demonstration of, 60–62
  discussion of model, 70–71
  guidelines, 58–59
  model of, 62–70
  reading for, 69–70
Culkin, Macaulay, 68

Databases, 40
Davis, Susan, 94
Descriptive passages, 7, 53
Discernment, 37
Documentation, 83, 104.
    *See also* Source materials
Draft and revision
  analysis writing, 167–169
  first, 8, 26–27, 83
  summary writing, 8, 26–27
  synthesis writing, 104
Drier, Peter, 145–147, 171

Economics assignments, 74
Either/or reasoning, 50
Emotionally loaded terms, 46–47
England, Lynndie R., 77–79
Entertaining writing, 53, 70
Essay exam, 3, 38, 71, 75, 147
Evaluation
  critical reading, 37
  entertaining writing, 53, 70
  informative writing, 39–41
  interpretation, 39, 40–41, 45–46
  persuasive writing, 70
Exam response
  comparison-and-contrast
    synthesis, 136–138
  comparison-and-contrast
    synthesis model, 132–136

  essay, 3, 38, 71, 75, 147
  explanatory synthesis model,
    140–142
Experimental reports, 146
Explanatory writing, 76–77, 79,
  80–81. *See also* Informative
  writing
  informative synthesis,
    138–144

Fair interpretation, 39, 40–41,
  45–46
False analogy, 51–52
The Family Educational Rights
  and Privacy Act (FERPA),
  95, 96–98
Faulty cause/effect, 48–49
FERPA. *See* The Family
  Educational Rights and
  Privacy Act
Fiction writing, 170
Film writing, 53
Financial principles, 162. *See also*
  Business planning
First draft, 8, 26–27
  synthesis writing, 83

Garfinkel, Harold, 159
Generalization, hasty, 50–51
Government assignment, 74
Government publication, 40
Grant proposal, 147
Greenberg, Harvey, 145–147, 171

Harrison, David, 105–115,
  116–121
Highlighting, 17–19
History assignment, 74

Imagination, 37
Information. *See also* Source
  materials
  accuracy of, 39, 40
  fair use of, for persuasion,
    39, 40–41, 45–46
  Internet, 40
  significance of, 39, 40

Informative writing, 69–70,
     76–81. *See also* Explanatory
     writing
   evaluation of, 39–41
   synthesis, 138–144
*An Inquiry into the Nature and
     Causes of the Wealth of Nations*
     (Smith), 11
Internet databases, 40
Interpretation, 39, 40–41, 45–46.
     *See also* Evaluation

Kaine, Tim, 94
Kazmierczak, Steven, 93
Keefer, Fredrika, 61–62
Key terms, 44–45
Kwan, Michelle, 67

Lab reports, 146
Legal argument, 3, 38, 147
Legitimacy of information, 40
Letter writing, 3, 74
Levin, Carl, 78
Library databases, 40
Literary analysis paper, 73, 147
Literature assignment, 3, 74
Literature review, 3, 74
Logical argumentation, 46–53, 125
Logical fallacies
   *ad hominem* argument, 47–48
   begging the question, 52
   either/or reasoning, 50
   emotionally loaded terms, 46–47
   false analogy, 51–52
   faulty cause/effect, 48–49
   hasty generalizations, 50–51
   *non sequitur*, 52
   oversimplification, 52–53

Magazine articles
   synthesis in, 74
   writing of, 80
Main points, 5
   key terms, 44–45
Malmon, Alison, 95
Medical chart, 3, 147

Memorandum, 3
   synthesis in, 74
"Military Abuse" (*Boston Globe*
     editorial), 78–79
MLA. *See* Modern Language
     Association
Modern Language Association
     (MLA), 104
Motivational appeal, 124
*The Movies on Your Mind*
     (Greenberg), 145–147, 171

Newspaper articles. *See also
     specific articles*
   synthesis in, 74, 76
*Non sequitur* (it does not follow), 52
Novel writing, 53

Organizational planning, 170
   analysis writing, 164–167
   climactic pattern, 124–125
   comparison-and-contrast syn-
     thesis, 128–130
   conventional pattern, 125
   synthesis writing, 83, 101–103
Oversimplification, 52–53
"Oz Was Almost Reality" (Drier),
     145–147, 171

Paraphrasing, 123–124. *See also*
     Quoted material
Patterns in organization
   climactic order, 124–125
   conventional, 125
   reading to identify, 170
Persuasive writing, 7, 47–52. *See
     also* Argument writing
   clearly defined terms, 44–45
   evaluation of, 70
   example of, 42–44
   fair use of information, 39,
     40–41, 45–46
   representative information, 46
Peselman, Edward, 151–157,
     165–167
Physics principles, 162

Plagiarism, 34–35, 104
avoiding, 36
Playwriting, 53
Poem writing, 53
Policy brief, 3, 38
synthesis in, 74
Political legislation, 40
Population data, 40
Position papers, 38
synthesis in, 74
"Private Gets 3 Years for Iraq
Prison Abuse" (Cloud), 77–78
Purpose identification
analysis writing, 157
argument synthesis, 82
primary, 38–39, 41–42, 69, 76, 81
synthesis writing, 73–75, 98–99

Quoted material. *See also* Source
materials
citations, 36
plagiarism, 34–36, 104
synthesis argument using,
123–124

Ralston, Eric, 62–70
Ratzinger, Joseph, 55
Reading process, 4–6. *See also*
Critical reading
for analysis writing, 158–161,
169–170
discovering relationships
via, 170
highlighting during, 17–19
involvement in, 37
note-taking during, 82
rereading, 17
Reasoning, 39–41, 70. *See also*
Logical fallacies
discernment, 37
either/or, 50
stages of thought, 19–20, 21–22
Reformulation, 83
Report paper, 3
Representative information, 46
Research paper, 3, 38, 73, 146

Resources, information, 40. *See
also* Source materials
Revision
analysis writing, 167–169
first draft and, 8, 25–26, 83
reformulation, 84
summary writing, 8, 26–27
synthesis writing, 104
Ryan, Joan, 42–44, 56–57, 60–61
Ralston's critique, 62–70

San Francisco Ballet Company,
56–57, 64–65
Sensitivity, 37
Seung Hui Cho, 88–92, 105–115
Associated Press article on,
93–95
Smith, Adam, 11
"Sociological Insight" (Collins),
157–161, 167
Sociological principles, 162
Sokolow, Bret, 95
Source materials, 101. *See also*
Information
accuracy of information, 39, 40
argument synthesis examples,
86–92
critical reading of, 72
documentation of, 83, 104
paraphrasing from, 123–124
plagiarism, 34–36, 104
synthesis writing using,
75–76, 83, 101
Stages of thought, 19–20
examples of summarizing,
21–22
Story writing, 53
Subordinate point, 6
Summary writing, 2–4, 27–31,
29–31
critical reading, 5–6, 37, 38
demonstration of, 8–16
explanation of, 1
final steps for, 31–32
first draft, 26–27

guidelines, 7–8
how to write, 7–8
length of, 32–33
of thesis, 23–26
Supportive evidence
synthesis argument, 123–124
Synthesis writing, 3, 74, 77–81, 85,
143–144
argument type of, 103–104,
121–123
comparison-and-contrast,
organizational plan for,
128–130
comparison-and-contrast type
of, 127–138
counterargument used in,
104, 126
defined, 72–73
demonstration of, 86–88
draft and revision of, 104
explanatory type of, 138–144
guidelines for, 81–84
Harrison's model of, 105–115,
116–121
informative, 138–144
organizational plan for, 83,
101–103
purpose identification in,
73–75, 98–99
as recursive process, 83–84
source materials for, 75–76,
83, 101
support for, 122–127
thesis formulation for, 99–101
types of, 81

Tension, in essay, 71
"The Coming Apart of a Dorm
Society" (Peselman),
151–157, 165–167
Thesis, 7, 42–52
analysis writing, 161–163
statement, 41

summary writing, 22–26
synthesis writing, 82
Topic sentences, 83
Transitions, 28
between paragraphs, 6
words/phrases for writing, 8
Trustworthy information, 40

Validity, 37
"Virginia Tech Massacre Has
Altered Campus Mental
Health Systems" (Associated
Press), 93–95

Wallace, David, 94
Warren, Robert Penn, 75
"We Are Not Created Equal in
Every Way" (Ryan), 42–44,
56–57, 60–61
critique of, 62–70
Web
databases, 40
sites, synthesis in, 74
Winn, Marie, 148–151, 158, 165
*Wizard of Oz* (Baum), 145–147, 171
Woods, Tiger, 66
Workplace writing
analysis in, 38
synthesis in, 74
Writing. *See also* Organizational
planning; *specific types*
author's purpose in, 38–39,
41–42, 69, 76, 81
college-level, 4
to entertain, 53, 70
identifying purpose of, 73–75,
81, 82, 98–99, 157
to inform, 39–41, 69–70,
76–81
main/subordinate points,
5–6, 44–45
to persuade, 7, 39–52, 70
for self knowledge, 59

# APA Documentation: Basic Formats

## APA In-text Citations

Place citation information—author, publication year, passage locator (page or paragraph number)—in sentence or in parentheses.

Summary or paraphrase—refer only to the year of publication:

> Berk (2002) suggested that many researchers view punishment as a quick fix.

Quotation—author and publication date *not* mentioned in sentence:

> A good deal of research suggests that punishing a child "promotes only momentary compliance" (Berk, 2002, p. 383).

Quotation—author and publication date mentioned in sentence:

> According to Berk (2002), a good deal of research suggests that punishing a child "promotes only momentary compliance" (p. 383).

## APA References List

At the end of the paper, on a separate page titled "References" (no italics or quotation marks), alphabetize sources by author, providing full bibliographic information for each. The most common entry types follow.

BOOK

### Basic entry

> Freud, S. (1920). *Dream psychology: Psychoanalysis for beginners* (M. D. Elder, Trans.). New York: James A. McCann.
> Freud, S. (1920). *Dream psychology: Psychoanalysis for beginners* (M. D. Elder, Trans.). Retrieved from http://www.gutenberg.org/etext/15489

### Selection from an edited book

> Halberstam, D. (2002). Who we are. In S. J. Gould (Ed.), *The best American essays* 2002 (pp. 124–136). New York: Houghton Mifflin.

### Later edition

> Samuelson, P., & Nordhaus, W. D. (2005). *Economics* (18th ed.). Boston: McGraw-Hill/Irwin.

ARTICLE FROM A MAGAZINE

> Davison, P. (2000, May). Girl, seeming to disappear. *Atlantic Monthly*, 108–111.
> Davison. P. (2000, May). Girl, seeming to disappear. *Atlantic Monthly*. Retrieved from http://www.theatlantic.com/issues/2000/05/davison.htm

Do not include retrieval date, when the source is unlikely to change.

ARTICLE FROM A JOURNAL ANNUAL VOLUME

> Ivanenko, A., & Massie, C. (2006). Assessment and management of sleep
> disorders in children. *Psychiatric Times, 23*(11), 90–95.
>
> Ivanenko, A., & Massie, C. (2006). Assessment and management of sleep
> disorders in children. *Psychiatric Times, 23*(11), 90–95. Retrieved from
> http://find.galegroup.com

In referencing an online text available only through a subscription service, provide the URL for the home page or menu page of the service.

Whether a journal article is paginated by issue or continuously through the annual volume, include both volume and issue number (if available) when citing the electronic version of the source.

ARTICLE FROM A NEWSPAPER

> Ridberg, M. (2006, May 4). Professors want their classes "unwired."
> *Christian Science Monitor,* p. 16.
>
> Ridberg, M. (2006, May 4). Professors want their classes "unwired."
> *Christian Science Monitor.* Retrieved from
> http://www.csmonitor.com/2006 /0504/pl6s01-legn.html

ARTICLE FROM THE INTERNET

> Weinberg, H. (n.d.). Group psychotherapy resource guide. Retrieved August
> 28, 2007, from http://www.group-psychotherapy.com/

If you think the online content might change, include the retrieval date.

# MLA DOCUMENTATION: BASIC FORMATS

## MLA In-text Citations

Use parentheses to enclose a page number reference to a source. Include the author's name if you do not mention it in your sentence:

> From the beginning, the AIDS antibody test has been "mired in controversy" (Bayer 101).

Omit the author's name from your in-text citation if mentioned in the sentence:

> According to Bayer, the AIDS antibody test has been "mired in controversy" (101).

## MLA Works Cited List

At the end of the paper, on a separate page titled "Works Cited," alphabetize each cited source by author's last name. Provide full bibliographic information, as shown. State how you accessed the source, via print or Web. Precede "Web" with a database name (e.g., LexisNexis) or the title of a Web site and a publisher.[1] Follow "Web" with your date of access. Note the use of punctuation and italics. Common entry types:

ARTICLE FROM A MAGAZINE

*Accessed via print*
> Packer, George. "The Choice." *New Yorker* 28 Jan. 2008: 28-35. Print.

*Accessed via Web (identical to print version)*
> Packer, George. "The Choice." *New Yorker* 28 Jan. 2008: n. pag.
> *NewYorker.com.* Web. 8 Nov. 2008.*

*Accessed via database (identical to print version)*
> Packer, George. "The Choice." *New Yorker* 28 Jan. 2008: n. pag. *Academic
> OneFile.* Web. 8 Nov. 2008.

*Article via Web (article exists on Web only; no print version)*
> Benjamin, Daniel. "The Mumbai Terrorists' Other Targets." *Slate.* Washington
> Post Newsweek Interactive, 1 Dec. 2008. Web. 4 Dec. 2008.

ARTICLE FROM A NEWSPAPER

*Accessed via print*
> Reynolds, Maura. "Recession Could Last into 2010." *Los Angeles Times*
> 2 Dec. 2008: A1+. Print.*

*Accessed via Web (identical to print version)*
> Reynolds, Maura. "Recession Could Last into 2010." *Los Angeles Times*
> 2 Dec. 2008: A1+. *LATimes.com.* Web. 2 Dec. 2008.

*Accessed via database (identical to print version)*
> Reynolds, Maura. "Recession Could Last into 2010." *Los Angeles Times*
> 2 Dec. 2008: A1+. *LexisNexis.* Web. 2 Dec. 2008.

*Accessed via Web (article exists on Web only; no print equivalent)*
> Brown, Campbell. "Plan for Bailout Money Doesn't Make Sense."
> *CNN.com.* Cable News Network, 4 Dec. 2008. Web. 4 Dec. 2008.

ARTICLE FROM A SCHOLARLY JOURNAL

*Accessed via print (include volume and issue numbers)*
> Ivanenko, Anna, and Clifford Massie. "Assessment and Management of Sleep
> Disorders in Children." *Psychiatric Times* 23.11 (2006): 90-95. Print.

[1]Exception: Online scholarly journal with no print equivalent. See below.

### Accessed via Web (identical to print version)

Ivanenko, Anna, and Clifford Massie. "Assessment and Management of Sleep Disorders in Children." *Psychiatric Times* 23.11 (2006): n. pag. *Psychiatrictimes.com.* Web. 3 Mar. 2009.*

### Accessed via database (identical to print version)

Ivanenko, Anna, and Clifford Massie. "Assessment and Management of Sleep Disorders in Children." *Psychiatric Times* 23.11 (2006): n. pag. *Academic OneFile.* Web. 3 Mar. 2009.

### Accessed via Web (article exists on Web only; no print equivalent)

Peterson, Karen. "Teens, Literature, and the Web." *The Alan Review* 31.3 (2004): n. pag. Web. 3 Mar. 2009.

#### BOOK

### Accessed via print

Fitzgerald, F. Scott. *This Side of Paradise.* New York: Scribner's, 1920. Print.

### Accessed via database

Fitzgerald, F. Scott. *This Side of Paradise.* New York: Scribner's, 1920. *Bartleby.com.* Web. 20 Oct. 2008.

### Selection from an anthology

Hardy, Melissa. "The Heifer." *The Best American Short Stories 2002.* Ed. Sue Miller. Boston: Houghton, 2002. 97-115. Print.*

### Second or subsequent edition

Whitten, Phillip. *Anthropology: Contemporary Perspectives.* 8th ed. Boston: Allyn, 2001. Print.*

#### WEB SITE

### Entire Web site

McMillan, Gail, dir. *Love Letters of the Civil War.* Va. Tech., 5 Mar. 2008. Web. 18 Dec. 2008.*

### Part of a Web site

Morris, J.C. "My Dear Amanda." 10 May 1863. Letter. *Love Letters of the Civil War.* Dir. Gail McMillan. Va. Tech., 5 Mar. 2008. Web. 18 Dec. 2008.

McGirt, Ellen. "The Minneapolis Bridge Collapse: Our Crumbling Infrastructure." *Fast Company.* Mansueto Ventures LLC, 2 Aug. 2007. Web. 12 Sept. 2008.

* MLA abbreviations include n.p. = no publisher or place of publication given; n.d. = no date given; n. pag. = no page(s) given—typical of sources found online; ed. = editor; ed. = edition; dir. = director; trans. = translator; comp. = compiler; + = non-consecutive pages beyond first listed. Capitalize the

# CHECKLIST FOR WRITING SUMMARIES (CHAPTER 1)

- **Read the passage carefully.** Determine its structure. Identify the author's purpose in writing.
- **Reread.** *Label* each section or stage of thought. *Highlight* key ideas and terms.
- **Write one-sentence summaries** of each stage of thought.
- **Write a thesis:** a one- or two-sentence summary of the entire passage.
- **Write the first draft** of your summary.
- **Check your summary** against the original passage.
- **Revise** your summary.

# CHECKLIST FOR WRITING CRITIQUES (CHAPTER 2)

- **Introduce** both the passage being critiqued and the author.
- **Summarize** the author's main points, making sure to state the author's purpose for writing.
- **Evaluate** the validity of the presentation.
- **Respond** to the presentation: agree and/or disagree.
- **Conclude** with your overall assessment.